FAR FROM PLAIN
Sailing

A book for those who have lost their way,
to inspire them to look towards a happier tomorrow
and to find the right path in life.

MEMOIRS
Cirencester

GW00683550

FAR FROM
PLAIN
Sailing

A book for those who have lost their way,
to inspire them to look towards a happier tomorrow
and to find the right path in life.

PHILLIPPA LESLIE

Published by Memoirs

MEMOIRS
PUBLISHING

25 Market Place, Cirencester, Gloucestershire, GL7 2NX
info@memoirsbooks.co.uk www.memoirspublishing.com

First published in England, 2009

Book jacket design Ray Lipscombe

ISBN 978-1-909544-40-6

Printed in England

To my children – Amanda, Carrie, Emma and Lucy – without whose love and support I doubt that I would have survived. To Juliana, who persevered where others would have given up, and Hazel, whose spiritual guidance was invaluable in establishing my identity and approach to life. I owe so much to my mother, who instilled in me a sense of purpose, the courage to face life as it comes, and to hold my head up high.

If there is one thing I have learned, it is that strength comes from knowing you are not alone – that it is not a sign of weakness to ask for help. On the contrary. It is the start of a new life and a brave, fresh beginning – the seed of success.

(Note: Names of some characters have been changed to protect their identities.)

Close your eyes for just one minute
And quieten down the world
Touch your soul, the strength that's in it
And love as yet unfurled
Clear your mind of constant chatter
Incessant nagging doubts
And tell yourself it doesn't matter
Dismiss the 'ins' and 'outs'
Calm the frenzy man's created
In pursuance of a dream
Gather in the warmth around you
Abundant in life's scheme
Open up your heart and listen
You'll find the answers there
For all the troubles now arisen
That lead you to despair
You're loved, protected, and a gift
To all who cry in pain
Be there to guide and spirits lift
Your heartaches aren't in vain

CHAPTER 1

My mother was tired when she died; exhausted by the continual struggle to overcome adversity and more than ready to finally submit to a God in whom she had placed unwavering faith and trust. To a non-believer it would seem that her God had failed her immeasurably, never seeming to answer her desperate pleas and prayers for peace and an end to her anguish. She accepted without question the agonies and disappointments that life had thrown at her, believing that all heart-breaking and seemingly impossible obstacles to surmount were 'character building', that God did not present us with anything that we could not rise above. She was emotionally and physically drained through drudgery, worrying and trying to make ends meet with nothing really to compensate. She was bringing up three children virtually on her own, as my father was usually away all day at work, and in the evenings, when supper was over, he would disappear to work on the current model he was making.

I rarely saw my mother sit down to rest during the day as she seemed always to be busy doing something. There were none of our modern conveniences such as washing machines, dryers etc., and she had no help, doing everything herself, down to mopping the floors, and wringing out the sheets. Always with an apron on, which only came off in the evenings when she sat down with us to listen to the radio – *Journey into Space*, *Dick Barton*, *The Navy Lark* and *Just a Minute* – all had an airing. Even that time was designated to sewing for us all and darning socks!

Life had not been what she had expected, and her husband had not turned out to be the provider that she had envisaged. Although he was physically a strong man, loving and dependable, he was lacking in drive, and it was she who pulled them through traumatic times by constantly encouraging him. Her own talents as an accomplished singer, pianist, artist, poet and linguist, in both French and German, went unrecognised. I think it was possibly a form of jealousy that kept him from ever praising her for her achievements or encouraging her in any venture, such as her poetry. The only poem that really appealed to him was one she wrote exclusively for him called 'Devon Man'. Her hair had gone completely white at an early age, which made her very attractive, immediately standing out in a crowd. She was a fashionable woman, with clear blue-grey eyes full of intelligence and laughter, and was popular with both men and women alike. She had an aura of quiet serenity and grace about her, though emotionally she was very strong, having considerable courage and tenacity.

My father was prone to the odd surprise however, such as arriving home one day with a beautiful new mangle to help her with the washing, I remember my brother turning the handle for her and getting his fingers caught in the cogs! Also, a new carpet turned up out of the blue. He was steadfast in his love for us all, though there were conflicting emotions where my brother was concerned.

It is only now that I can look back and see how it really was, and how they both suffered in different ways; my father the humiliation of not being able to give my mother the life she should have had, and silently enduring the proffered help from her family, and my mother for the drastic change in lifestyle she underwent when she married him. However, as far as I was concerned, he was a very loving father. He took little part in actually bringing me up, but he was always there in the background, solid as a rock, and spoiling me whenever possible. He was the strong, silent type, and my grandfather (my mother's father) referred to him as 'the man who only speaks on Tuesdays'! He had a great capacity for love, though this love bordered on possessiveness.

I was born in Taunton, Somerset in 1944, the youngest of three children, with a seven-year gap between each of us. My sister, Janet, was thirteen and my brother Timothy seven when I arrived. I come from a mixture of backgrounds, my mother descended from a well-respected Scottish family, while my father's roots were ultimately in Devon, his father having been a country doctor. His family tree has been in our family for many years, and we are able to trace it back to the 1600s when a French smuggler, Ambrose le Gros, sailed across the English Channel to trade along the Cornish coast.

My father had had a very sad and lonely childhood, losing his mother through cancer when she was very young, and he and his sister had been brought up by a spinster aunt who cared little for children and their need for love. His mother, however, passed on to him the wonderful talent of being able to make anything with his hands. She had carved the most beautiful articles of furniture out of oak, such as her husband's surgery desk and chair, mirrors and all the heavy oak furniture that graced my home as a child. She must have been a very unusual and remarkable person, as this was an extraordinary pastime for a woman in that era. The children both must have been lost when she suddenly died at the age of thirty-eight. Their father, being a doctor, had little time to spare to pay much attention to their upbringing.

My mother had a gentle upbringing in Calcutta, India, where she was born, until the age of seven when she was sent to boarding school in England, along with her sister Helen and three brothers Andrew, Alec and Crawford. On leaving school at the age of eighteen she returned to India, and I would listen with fascination to stories of her escapades and of her social engagements. When I was little I played with her opera glasses, calling cards and dance cards, which had little pencils attached to them. She would become quite animated and her eyes would shine when she spoke of the many tea dances and balls she and Helen had attended at Government House in Calcutta, the dates they had had and how her father had bought them both fur coats, a dark brown mink for Helen and a light grey for my mother (not so acceptable now of course).

4

I also heard how Helen refused to marry a young man who pleaded with her to do so outside her bedroom window. My poor (and lovely) aunt never married, bitterly regretting not having said 'Yes' to her Kenneth, especially after reading in the paper that he had married someone else, and much later was devastated to read in the obituaries that he had died and gone for ever. I think she thought that as long as he was alive he was there for her, and literally gave up after having read this. She very rapidly went downhill health-wise and died tragically, long before my mother.

My mother too had had offers of marriage but refused. She was dubbed the 'butterfly' of the family, having a naturally happy disposition, loving to sing, dance and play the piano and ukulele, which she often did at parties. This is not to say she was uncaring. She was a very loving and sensitive person, with a gentle nature and a sense of fun. She spoke of her passage on the liner out to India – of dinners on board with the captain and dances and fancy-dress balls. Madame Pompadour and Pierrot were two of the many costumes they donned for these occasions, and how romantic it all was.

One of the models my father made was of the liner *Edinburgh Castle* in which he installed lights. This model was in our drawing room at home, and at night he would turn the main lights off and the lights in the little ship would twinkle and shine on the decks and through the portholes. It looked beautiful, and my mother would be transported back to those ocean-going days of romance and excitement. He also put a night sky behind it with a moon and stars – it was magical. He was so clever with his hands and made anything any of us requested. One of his most beautiful creations was a wedding present for me in the form of a galleon in full sail made out of silver with copper sails, every delicate and intricate detail and every item of rigging made by hand.

My mother spoke lovingly of her own mother, Emma Helen Leslie, who was of a similarly gentle disposition, totally devoted to all her five children and a long-suffering wife to my grandfather, Franklin Marston Leslie, whom I gather was rather fond of the ladies, and caused her many sleepless nights! Being in the family law firm of Leslie and Hinds in Calcutta, he was in the rather cosy position of being able to comfort many a would-be divorcee, though while ill and dying he looked into my grandmother's eyes and said 'It was only ever you, Em'.

It must have broken my grandmother's heart when the time came for them all in turn to be educated in England, especially Marjorie, my mother, who was only seven years old and Helen, who was only nine. In those days this was the 'done thing' for all well-to-do British families in India, and what they all went through as a result of this cannot be imagined. This self-inflicted sentence is hard to envisage from the parents' point of view. Eleven years without seeing one's children, except on very rare occasions, must have been unbearable, and from the children's point of view it must have left them feeling totally abandoned.

They went to boarding school in Bristol at Clifton College, with the boys I believe going to the same school but obviously a different building. Helen of course looked after my mother as best she could, but their holidays were usually spent apart, with each going to separate friends. My grandmother religiously wrote to each of them in turn every week.

However, it must have been a wonderful feeling when the time came for Helen and my mother to leave school and return to India, when at last they could be a family again. Andrew, Alec and Crawford, as far as I know, had enlisted and were all in the army and fighting in the First World War, all coming through it safely and returning to Calcutta and the family, Alec having been wounded and receiving the Military Cross. My grandfather, Franklin Leslie, served under British Field Marshal Lord Clyde who raised the siege of Lucknow, capturing Cawnpore during the Indian Mutiny. He, at that time, held the rank of lieutenant and was then attached to the 53rd Native Infantry, having been awarded Medal and Clasp. A portrait of him hangs in the British Library in London, where there is also a rather beautiful painting of my great-grandfather Sheppard Leslie's somewhat grand home Combermere Lodge on the river at Barrackpore, built on the lines of an Italian palace, with horse-artillery cannon in the foreground, linked together with their trace chains.

My grandmother was the first woman on a bicycle in Calcutta, which caused quite a stir among the locals, and she was a pioneer in many ways. One example was her very daring expedition into the Himalayas with just a girlfriend for company (always referred to as 'Miss Jacob'!) and *syces* (grooms) to tend to the horses and to carry their supplies. She wrote a diary of her journey which appears at the end of this book. It is so old and so beautifully written that I think it deserves to be seen. She came from Dutch missionary stock, and I imagine the quest for adventure was in her blood. Her father, Henry Bawn Addis, was a railway engineer co-designing the Darjeeling Himalayan Railway, her maternal grandfather having been a missionary in India. Her mother was of Dutch extraction, being a descendant of the Van Someren family, and I remember having a rather lovely Aunt Lottie (Charlotte van Someren) who lived in London and once took me to the Natural History Museum and Madame Tussaud's when I was about seven! I assume, at this rather late stage, that she was a cousin of my grandmother. Their history can be traced back to the 1750s to the birth of Peter van Someren, who was a Dutch free mariner for the Dutch East India Company.

My grandparents' house in Calcutta was of Colonial style, surrounded by palms and shrubs, with servants' quarters and a stable block accommodating six to eight horses. There was an abundance of Indian servants to see to all aspects of running a home. To have servants in India was the norm, almost all British families having a large number. This was mainly due to the 'caste' system whereby each servant had his or her individual duty and was forbidden to interfere with another, the higher the 'caste' the more important (and cleaner!) the job. The *sahib*'s (master of the house) bearer looked after his clothes and kept the household bills in order;

the *memsahib*'s (mistress) *ayah* took on similar duties for her mistress, but she would not touch any sewing, this job being done by the *dirzi*. The cooking was done by the *kansamah* who was on call day or night; the *khidmatgar* waited at table, but would not touch any washing up or handle any wet cutlery etc. The *bheesti* fetched and carried the water and saw to people's baths. There was an *ayah* for the children, *syces* for the horses and *jhampanis* to draw the rickshaw. A *punkah wallah* sat on the veranda operating the fans, and the *chowkidar* was the night watchman. A *dhobi* attended to the washing and ironing. So, as you can imagine, with everyone doing their individual jobs the household was run very smoothly, the servants themselves being only too happy to be in constant employment. Also, in the Leslie household they were treated with great fondness and respect, my mother and her siblings picking up the native Hindustani language from the servants as a matter of course.

During the rainy season the family were confined to the house, and the days were really rather boring for young children, apart from the odd trip out on a flooded lawn in a rowing boat! The water swirled around the house at a considerable depth, and these escapades were a lot of fun. The two younger boys, Alec and Crawford, Helen and my mother paddled happily about for hours – supervised by their *ayah*. To pass the time on one occasion, when they were much older, my grandmother got out an ouija board for entertainment. They all sat round the table and started asking it questions. One of the questions asked was 'Where is Andrew?'

Apparently the children's older brother was supposed to be on his way home from England and they hadn't yet heard from him. The board spelt out 'CASS'. This was rather baffling – until the following day they had a telegram from Andrew saying he would be arriving the next day with his new fiancée. He duly arrived, and introduced his fiancée Cassandra – Cass for short! They were totally dumbfounded and considerably shaken, and my grandmother forbade any further use of the board. Subsequently, Andrew was tragically killed in a motorbike accident very soon after, leaving his young wife pregnant with their unborn son, my cousin Andrew.

On my mother's return to Calcutta at eighteen (as part of the 'fishing fleet') a very different life awaited her from that of being confined to the rigours of a strict boarding school environment. Life in India was idyllic, both the climate and the lifestyle. Their days (hers and Helen's) were mostly spent horse-riding, playing golf, attending tennis parties, fancy-dress parties (I have a lovely photo of her dressed as a 'vamp'), and meeting up for coffee, tea or dinner at Firpo's on Chowringhee, the city's fashionable restaurant at which the glitterati of Calcutta entertained themselves and their friends. I can remember her using phrases such as 'lounge lizards', 'poodle-fakers' and 'co-respondent shoes'! All these pertaining to the men of the time and their rather effeminate or suspect behaviour! She herself was absolutely chaste until the day she married my father (or so she told me).

My grandfather once put my mother on his very high-spirited horse Black Douglas – I'm sure to test her mettle! During the ride something must have frightened him, or perhaps he just felt like playing up, as he took off at a break-neck gallop. My mother, who usually rode side-saddle (Helen always rode astride), hung on for dear life for what seemed like hours, with Helen shouting 'stick it kid' from far behind her! She managed not to fall off, but it was nevertheless a very frightening and unsettling experience. She usually rode her mother's horse, Redwing. However, even her mother had experienced a dreadful accident on her own horse when it became frightened by something on Calcutta race course, and it threw her on to some railings. One of the spikes glanced off her head, causing her very severe headaches in the future. My mother said she quite frequently left them to lie down in a darkened room when having one of these attacks.

At tennis parties my mother always said she was very feeble, and the boys used to say she had arms like bits of tape! Being the youngest, she was the butt of family teasing from the boys, and I remember her telling me that on the eve of her birthday Alec told her that 'tomorrow never comes'! She was definitely not the sporty type, with which I can sympathize, as I am very much the same. She and Alec used to partner each other and virtually 'take over' the dance floor, mainly doing the Charleston! A bit of an exhibitionist, my Mum – I know where I get it from! She was presented to the Viceroy (representative of the British Crown in India) together with Helen and my grandmother, at a ball held at Government House in Calcutta, at which it was intended that the two girls should meet 'suitable' husband material!

The family had a bungalow up in the hills in Shillong, to which they moved during the summer months when it became too hot in Calcutta. Whilst in the bungalow one season, Helen became dangerously ill with '*spru*', the local term for a form of dysentery. I don't know at which point they decided to leave India and come home, but this would seem to be a feasible one. Helen had beautiful dark brown hair reaching well past her waist, and when she had it cut, it was made into a switch with which I had great fun dressing up, putting it underneath my mother's hats! Oddly enough, I can remember vividly a lullaby my mother sang to me in Hindustani when I was very small, and one which had been sung to her by her *ayah* when she too was little:

Nini baba, nini,
Muckan, roti, cheeni,
Roti, muckan hogya,
Hamara baba sogya!

(Sleep baby sleep, butter, bread, sugar, the bread and butter are finished, my baby's asleep!)

There are two conflicting versions of the following events. One was told me by my cousin Rosemary, and one was told by my mother, the first account being that on their decision to leave, my grandfather's wish was that Crawford take over the family business. Crawford refused, and the most awful row ensued where my grandfather literally banished him from the house – not only that but my grandfather insisted he leave the family altogether and start a separate life in Australia. The other version is by far the worst that could have happened in those times, this being that Crawford had got a girl into trouble, and had been punished accordingly. What might have happened to the girl is not known! The whole family was in shock, but my grandfather would not be swayed. Crawford boarded a ship bound for Australia and was never seen by any of the family again. This does not seem a terribly honourable thing to have done, and perhaps this story is not true! He married an Australian girl and became head chef in a good hotel in Melbourne. He rarely wrote to my mother, but they did keep in touch, and I remember one Christmas day, about thirty years later, she got a phone call from him. I've never seen her look so happy – it was a thrilling moment for her. The rest of the family came home to England and took a house in Surbiton, Surrey.

Alec eventually took over the family business, married twice (my cousin Rosemary being from his first marriage and now living in Australia) and stayed out in Calcutta until 1965 when he became very ill and died in Westminster Hospital, London. He and his wife Christine used to occasionally come home on 'leave', which was always very exciting, especially for my mother and me, and he would always bring presents of some kind. I remember a beautiful little set of graduated ivory elephants that he gave me one year, which sadly I have now lost in various house moves.

During the early twentieth century women came into their own, casting aside the shackles of being 'kept' by their husbands and treated as simpering, brainless individuals, not capable of logical thought! They demonstrated for their right to vote and to take their rightful place in society, financially supporting themselves, therefore making them independent of their husbands. Hence the Suffragettes were born, with Emmeline Pankhurst one of the foremost and most prominent agitators in their quest for freedom, and a name we are all familiar with.

The move for women to have the vote had really started in 1897 when Millicent Fawcett founded the National Union of Women's Suffrage. She was concerned that any violence would persuade men that women could not be trusted to have the right to vote, but this plan was soon to prove ineffectual, though it was the forerunner of the more extreme Suffrage movement. In 1903 the Women's Social and Political Union was founded by Emmeline Pankhurst and her daughters Christabel and Sylvia. They wanted women to have the right to vote and were not prepared to wait. The union became known as the Suffragettes, members of which were prepared to use violence to get what they wanted.

Emmeline Pankhurst later wrote in her autobiography, 'this was the beginning of a campaign the like of which was never known in England, or for that matter in any other country, we interrupted a great many meetings and we were violently thrown out and insulted. Often we were painfully bruised and hurt.' They burned down churches as the Church of England was against what they wanted; they vandalized Oxford Street, breaking all the windows in the street; they chained themselves to Buckingham Palace as the royal family were seen to be against women having the right to vote; they hired boats, sailed up the Thames and shouted abuse through loud-hailers at Parliament as it sat; others refused to pay their tax. Politicians were attacked on their way to work, their homes being set on fire. Golf courses were vandalized. Suffragettes were quite happy with being imprisoned and they refused to eat, going on hunger strike. The prison governors were ordered to force-feed them. When those who had been arrested and later released had regained their strength, they were rearrested for very trivial reasons and the whole process started again. As a result of this their acts became more extreme, and at the June Derby at Epsom in 1913 Emily Davison threw herself under King George V's horse. She was killed instantly, becoming the Suffragette's martyr. In the same year they blew up politician David Lloyd George's house. However, in 1914 Britain was plunged into World War One and their campaign came to a stop, with instructions from Emmeline Pankhurst to give vital support in every way to the government and the war effort, women then playing an extremely important role in the field of conflict and back home. In 1918 the Representation of the

People Act was passed by Parliament and the battle for equality was won!

During World War Two women also played a vital part in the ferrying of all kinds of planes around England for the Air Transport Auxiliary. They flew Spitfires, Hurricanes and Lancasters unarmed, without radios or instruments, at the mercy of the weather and long-range enemy aircraft. They were nick-named the Powder Puff Pilots! Although many of them died when their aircraft developed engine trouble, they were able to fly every bit as well as the men, but did not receive the recognition they deserved. Probably the most famous member of the ATA was Amy Johnson who joined in 1940. In 1941 she was killed in the Thames Estuary after flying from a base in north England in very poor weather. What happened to her and her plane remains a mystery.

My own mother decided it was time that she asserted her own brand of emancipation and began scouring the daily papers for suitable positions for a woman of gentle disposition. However, it was actually at a dinner party that she was approached by the Ambassador of Foreign Affairs. He offered to introduce her to the Rani of Jaipur who, ensconced in the Savoy Hotel with her husband the Rajah, happened to be looking for a companion. She happily accepted the position, commuting to and from work from Surbiton on the tube. Her job consisted of reading to the Rani, running little errands, teaching her to dance, also banking extremely large amounts of money, which made her very nervous, having to cross

London in taxis in fear of being mugged, if anyone found out exactly how much she was carrying. This position lasted several months but unfortunately had to come to an end when the sight of the Rani chasing the Rajah round the hotel with a rolled-up umbrella became too much for my mother, plus the fact that the Rajah became rather amorous and asked her to teach him to dance! Not really what she had had in mind. She sadly had to leave, much to the regret of the Rani who had become very fond of her, so much so that she gave her a beautiful emerald ring from her finger as a parting gift and a thank you for having done her job so well. It was after this, with her confidence in her independence boosted, that she opened a dance studio in Knightsbridge, teaching ballroom dancing.

It may seem odd, but I have always thought that I am in the wrong era! Not only the wrong era but the wrong country! I know that I should be far happier in a hotter and friendlier country, and I would have fitted rather nicely into my mother's existence in Calcutta in the 'roaring twenties' when most families were reasonably secure and grounded, where manners were seldom brought to account, chivalry an accepted norm and life for the young revolved around tennis parties, golf, horse riding, dinner parties, theatre, music and dance! It was a wonderful time for the young who were not terribly concerned with the politics of the time, not realizing the implications the occupation of their country had on the native population, thinking that the party would go on for ever.

CHAPTER 2

My mother had made friends with a girl at her school called Enid, who came from Devon, and on leaving India still kept in touch. One summer, several old school friends met up for a picnic whilst on holiday in Devon, Enid bringing her rather good-looking brother along. This was her first introduction to my father, and she obviously fell in love with him virtually on sight, as they were married quite soon after in Surbiton.

Her life changed dramatically overnight from a comfortable, carefree existence to one of constant financial worry, and as a result she went through some agonizing and traumatic times. My father was at that time studying at Seale-Hayne Agricultural College in Devon to become a farmer. Having qualified during their engagement it was decided that they should try their luck at building a farming life for themselves in Australia. On arrival in Australia after a long sea voyage, he and a friend from college attempted to clear land sufficient for cultivation, but in the end found it was impossible to achieve, the bush being too dense, and that to attempt to farm there would have been a mammoth and back-breaking task, and the life too hard for my mother. They came home, very disappointed after all their hard work, having lost a considerable amount of weight! My parents moved to Southampton where my father obtained a job as a model-maker with Scott Paine. For example, he built the Schneider Trophy for presentation to the directors among other prototypes, and once made a model in ice for an exhibition. My sister, Janet, was born during this time.

However, the pull towards farming became too strong for my father to ignore; he had, after all, been trained for this purpose. On the death of his father both he and his sister were left a cottage each in Weare Gifford in Devon. Father sold his and with the proceeds they started up a farm in Chittlehamholt in Devon. My poor mother, having been brought up with servants, had no idea how to even boil an egg when they first married, and now suddenly had to become a farmer's wife. She had a cook book in one hand and a baby book in the other! I remember her saying to me 'Never let yourself go darling'. I know she never did throughout all the traumas she experienced. Her lipstick was always applied and her hair always in place, her appearance always neat and tidy. We children were also scrubbed and well turned out.

My mother has been the inspiration in my life, and would always make me feel as though I were here for a purpose. Having lived a life of perpetual disappointments and tragic outcomes, she instilled in me the will to survive, to know my own courage and abilities. Without her encouragement I doubt I would have maintained the optimistic outlook that I possess, and one that has got me through so many traumatic events in my life. In her jewellery box she had a pewter crest badge with a griffin on it, and the motto 'Grip Fast', given to her by her father. This is the Leslie family crest, and one to which she must often have referred in her life, and one that I now adhere to! The signet ring she always wore was a constant reassuring reminder of the strong family that she came from; a family that had been in existence for almost one thousand years, dating back to King Malcolm III Canmore of Scotland, whose sister Princess Beatrix married Bartholomew, a Hungarian nobleman to whom the king granted the lands of Leslie in Fife, Scotland in 1070. The king had promised Bartholomew, in hereditary right, all the lands within the radius of one mile of any point where he had to rest or feed his horse during one day's ride. He started north from Dunfermline stopping first at Fythkill in Fife, now known as Leslie, and after four more stops the horse finally expired in the lush pastures of the Garioch district. On his return to Dunfermline when the King asked how he had fared Bartholomew replied 'Between the lesse ley and the mair, my horse it tyrd and stopped there'. The king supposedly replied, 'Lord Lesse-ley shalt thou be and all thine heirs after thee'. (*Lesse* means sheltered and *ley* means pasture.) All subsequent Leslies are descended from Bartholomew.

In 1282 Norman de Lesly is said to have acquired lands at Fythkill, and a hundred years after that, Sir George Leslie and his new bride, Elizabeth Hay, the king's niece, were granted the barony of Fythkill in 1396. The annual rent was a pair of gloves! In 1457 George, 1st Earl of Rothes, from whom my family descends, was granted the barony of Leslie in Fife, and this is the first mention of the name of the place as Leslie.

John, 7th Earl, had been a staunch supporter of King Charles against Oliver Cromwell and after the Restoration (1660) the king rewarded him with several high offices, including that of Lord High Chancellor of Scotland for life. He was a highly cultured person with a good knowledge of art and architecture, and as he was now wealthy, he commissioned the building of a large and sumptuous country mansion. He employed a well-known Italian architect to draw up the plans, which included a large formal garden. The house was to be after the style of the royal palace at Holyrood, in Edinburgh, his gallery being three feet longer than the one at Holyrood. Everything, including the furniture, was totally luxurious.

The glory lasted 91 years. On Christmas day 1763 a disastrous fire destroyed virtually the whole house. Previously, it had suffered some damage by the Jacobites during the 'Fifteen', which was restored by the 9th Earl, and the 10th Earl had added some improvements. On that fateful Christmas day the house had some 80 rooms, containing a fine collection of furniture and paintings, and the library was said to be one of the finest in Scotland. The fire broke out during the night in a bad snow-storm, which severely hampered any effective fire-fighting. Some pictures were saved but otherwise it was almost a complete loss. The library was destroyed, most of the furniture, the family silver and many important documents and old charters were lost for ever. The 10th Earl, who was home for the Christmas holiday, supervised the fire-fighting efforts personally, but to little effect, as the fierce wind fanned the flames. The house that stands today is the West Wing, the only part that could be saved.

There are several Leslie castles and country houses, such as Ballinbreich on the shoreline of the River Tay, Balgonie Castle (occupied by Rob Roy MacGregor and two hundred Highlanders during the 1715 Stuart uprising), Pitcaple Castle in the Garioch, Balquain Castle close to the River Urie (some are in ruins but others are still lived in), mostly in Scotland. There is one famous castle in Ireland that most people will have heard of, being Castle Leslie, Glaslough, Co. Monaghan where Paul McCartney and Heather Mills were married. Sir John Leslie and his niece Samantha now run it as a hotel and equestrian centre.

In the year 1297 Sir Norman Leslie fought the English alongside the young knight William Wallace who, within a matter of weeks, became leader of an armed national force with his friend and companion Sir Andrew de Moray as deputy commander. This 'Army of the Commons of Scotland', as distinguished from a royal army (as Scotland had no king), was made up of the lesser nobility such as Sir Norman Leslie, farmers, and Gaelic-speaking people from the mountains and islands. Wallace and his troops won a decisive victory over the English at Stirling Bridge in the same year. Nine dreadful years of fighting followed with many deaths on both sides, Scotland being ravaged by the English. In 1305 Wallace was captured and taken to London; and after a very swift trial was condemned to death by being hung, drawn and quartered. His head was set on a pike above London Bridge, his right leg nailed above Berwick's town gate, the other in Perth, a third part placed in an open sewer in Newark and the fourth exposed in Aberdeen. It was a pretty ghastly way to go.

Quite interesting is the fact that Sir Norman Leslie was one of the great barons of Scotland who sat in the Parliament called by King Robert the Bruce in 1314. In 1320 his son, Andrew, the 6th Lord Leslie, was one of the signatories on the Declaration of Arbroath, a call to freedom not equalled again anywhere in the world until the American Declaration of Independence. With his sons began the spread of the family through several branches.

The original line died out with Andrew's grandson, but Walter, another son, became the Earl of Ross and John, another son, was the progenitor of the Earls of Rothes, while his brother, George, became the first Baron of Balquain.

To get back to the farm. The odds seemed continuously to be against my father where farming was concerned. He built chicken runs, cow sheds, pig sties, everything himself, only to lose it all during the slump of 1937. My mother said that that period was completely soul-destroying. They would get the cows milked early, the churns filled and put out for the Co-operative 'collecter' on the milk stand in the lane, only to find that they were still sitting there, in the sun, into mid-afternoon, by which time the milk was deemed unfit to process or be collected and was poured down the drain! They eventually had to declare themselves bankrupt, much to my father's shame, my mother having to pass on the family silver for safe keeping to the local doctor, who offered his help, before the bailiffs could take it, but they obviously took everything else that was of any value. This was a dreadfully worrying time for them both, particularly my mother, who had just given birth to my brother Tim when this disaster struck. During this traumatic episode, Tim became seriously under-nourished to the point where the doctor insisted he should be admitted to hospital or they would lose him.

I wonder how much of 'farming' my mother actually enjoyed. In those days a woman followed her man. Whatever his job, she acquiesced into playing a supporting role in his chosen career, whatever that might have been. I think she always made the best of it, being totally unselfish, though to have come from her genteel background to the backbreaking slog of keeping a farm going must surely have been a tremendous culture shock to say the least. I can imagine that she very rarely complained, but inside she must sometimes have felt despair and isolation.

There was one rather amusing episode, however. Having an apple orchard on the farm my father made cider, which was left to ferment in barrels in the barn. He also had a farm labourer in the form of Tyzack who performed the milking and general duties, helping with ploughing etc. However, after a morning's strenuous effort and a substantial lunch made by my mother, Tyzack could then be found, without fail, in the barn, snoring thunderously, passed out, his head inches from the gentle dripping of the barrel tap! My father hadn't the heart to sack him as in actual fact Tyzack was an extremely solid worker when not the worse for wear. A rather alarming occurrence happened when my father was carrying out the usual morning milking. My mother said he came through the kitchen door visibly shaking and as white as a sheet. Apparently a cow had taken fright whilst my father was filling the hay-racks and had reared up, coming down on top of him, its hooves pinning him across the rack. Farming can be a dangerous game!

After the heart-breaking failure of the farm, my parents moved to Taunton in Somerset, where my mother's parents and sister Helen were then living. They were lucky enough to obtain the house next door, which must have been very reassuring for my mother, to have her family so close after such a harrowing time.

My father worked throughout the war as an inspector of small parts for aeronautical navigational equipment in a local factory. During this time he was an active member of the Home Guard. He also worked as an experimental engineer for de Havilland Aircraft Co. in the 1950s, working on the 'Blue Streak' rocket. This was 'top secret', talk of which was not permitted, so my mother never really knew what he actually did. After World War Two new weapons were being invented.

Nuclear, and the new types of chemical and biological weapons, were obvious choices for the warheads of such delivery systems. However, the whole project was abandoned before any serious construction was done. It seems that the missile was going to be obsolete before it was deployed and the political will was not there to continue with the huge cost for no reason. The continuance of the nuclear deterrent was considered essential, but a more suitable system was sought.

Our education was mostly funded by my uncle Alec. He paid for Jan to go to a private school in Taunton and my brother to a public school, King's College, in Taunton, but not before Tim had suffered the humiliation of cycling round the back streets to attend a state school first. He was very ashamed of it and totally miserable, so Alec came to the rescue. He paid my fees when I started at a private school, 'The Beehive', at the age of five, but I was so unhappy I had to be taken away. The school was run by two spinster sisters who seemed to have a penchant for the boys, and the girls were a rather unwelcome but necessary addition. Being rather shy and very sensitive, I think I must have been an easy target for their sarcasm and rather archaic methods. I remember we were not allowed to go to the loo during lessons, and I got so anxious about this that accidents started happening, and in the end my poor sister had literally to drag me to school screaming! Needless to say, I was taken away from there and given a governess for a while. I was also given an IQ test by a psychologist to see if there was anything amiss, but this turned out to be above average. I was later put into another smaller private school, which was run by a retired naval captain, Captain Tanton. He was a lovely kind man, and I did very well there, being the one to show the new children the ropes and take them to the loo! I won several prizes for good work and good behaviour, which obviously was a relief to my parents, and most of all to Alec I should think, as he was paying for it all.

However, this unfortunately had to come to an end when I was ten, and I was then integrated into the system by attending a state school. By this time I had had a fairly solid grounding and was reasonably all right.

I had a walk of about a mile to reach my school, through rather unfriendly terrain! I took a short cut which ran beside the River Tone, but not before having to cross a really forbidding looking bridge over a weir. It was made of concrete with parallel tubular railings set roughly two feet apart. When covered with snow and ice in the winter this bridge was quite terrifying. You had to walk gingerly across it, very much aware that if you slipped it would possibly mean going under the bottom rail into the raging torrent that was the weir underneath! (I have since visited Taunton and found that they have now put wire netting over the rails, which is certainly an improvement!) When the snow had melted the river would be in flood and the toffee-coloured water raged over the falls, spewing cream spray several feet into the air, the level of the water very nearly touching the underside of the bridge, making one even more terrified, and the noise became a deafening roar. I was very nervous of my journeys to and from school in the winter.

Having conquered the bridge, my walk across the park was an eerie experience, with very often thick fog hanging over the water, the only sounds to be heard were the dripping of the dense fog off the trees and the thundering of the weir, not to mention the fact that I seemed to be the only one going home this way – a very lonely experience, except for the swans on the river, and one that would never be allowed these days. However, in the summer it was a different matter altogether. Ducks and swans swam on the river, with their families of small offspring paddling frantically behind in the wake of their mothers, the blossom on the chestnut trees and the carpet of lush grass across the park on which we held our sports day events. Although the sound of the weir was constant, it seemed not to hold the same menace as in the winter months.

I had a very traumatic experience when I was eight, which affected me for the rest of my life, and made me feel that I was different from everyone else. I had been looking after a little boy of three who lived just down the road. He was the son of a friend of my sister's, and I often went over to their house to play with him and keep an eye on him. This particular day I was tidying up his toys for the night, putting them in the shed, when his grandfather followed me in. A feeling of unease came over me immediately, as I knew he had no reason to be there. This was my first encounter with sexual abuse, and was not to be the last. When the shock of it began to sink in, I realized I had to get out and I ran home arriving in a hysterical state. My parents managed to get out of me what had happened, and were naturally horrified. Because I was so young, it was decided that I should not be subjected to a court appearance – instead, the family concerned moved away. There was another instance when I was ten, again involving someone I knew. In between these two incidents, however, was to be something that shattered my life for ever.

It was 1953, Coronation year of Queen Elizabeth II, and a hot Saturday afternoon in July. My brother Tim and a friend had managed to get hold of some gunpowder (unknown to either set of parents), and were trying to create bangs loud enough to frighten the neighbours. They had already caused one explosion that had made one of the neighbours drop the rabbit she was skinning, and they thought this hilarious. Tim was screwing the top onto an old cocoa tin, in order to make a repeat performance, when the whole thing exploded. I was playing with a friend down the road, and I can remember the noise it made, though I took no notice of it at the time. I could not have known that it had taken the life of my beloved brother, and only realized the full horror of it the following day. He was only sixteen years old – and in a month would have reached his seventeenth birthday.

My parents didn't actually tell me what had happened until the following morning, when I was sitting between them in their big double bed eating marmalade sandwiches and drinking my milk, which my father used to get as a Sunday morning treat instead of a formal breakfast. My brother, I knew, was not there that morning as I had already been told that he had been taken to hospital. I did not know until that moment that he was never coming back. I sat between them, my mother's comforting arm around me, numb as the horror of it sank in, the tears pouring down my cheeks and the sandwich stuck in my throat. My father was unable to speak. His relationship with Tim had been a rocky one, and I'm sure this played a part in his reaction to his death. He must have felt dreadful remorse for the way he had treated Tim. They were constantly rowing, there being a definite clash of personalities. I also think my father was jealous of my mother's love for him, and his general happy and carefree demeanour, my father's own childhood having been so different.

The day of the funeral I was sent away to Weymouth with one of my friends and her parents. I remember sitting on the beach feeling disorientated and unreal, as though it were all a dream, and wondering why I was there and not at home. Tim was hardly ever mentioned again, and certainly not in connection with me. It sometimes felt as though I'd never had a brother, and it all became dreadfully distant and detached. I think I knew that to mention him would upset my mother, so I never could. Because it seemed to be unacceptable to show one's feelings over anything remotely traumatic, I suppose I just went along with it as being the 'way people behaved'. It was not until I was much older that it really hit home, and I began to grieve inwardly, so much so that I became almost obsessed with wanting to know if he was all right. That may sound a bit strange but his going was so shockingly sudden that I felt it must have been very traumatizing for him too.

How would you be now – tall and strong
There for me when things go wrong
Laughing eyes and full of fun
To snuggle close when day is done
A hand to hold in a crowded street
Teasing boy with heart so sweet
How could you go and leave me here
With all my heart I wish you near
The wound is deeper now by far
And I often wonder where you are
Are you watching – do you see
How much your going meant to me
Your tender life had just begun
When you flew too close to the tempting sun

I was sometimes a lonely child, but with the death of my brother, it suddenly felt as though I were an only child. His going changed my life overnight and I knew I had been through an experience that my friends could not possibly understand or handle with ease, making me feel yet more isolated. Tim had only just left school and started his career as a trainee aeronautical engineering draughtsman with Westlands Aircraft in Yeovil. As a small child I can remember going into my brother's bedroom and being fascinated by the collection of aeroplanes lining the shelves and hanging from the ceiling. Tim had made them himself out of balsa wood and tissue paper, and a beautiful red one hung in the middle of the room. We had only just settled him into his digs a few weeks before, and been so sad to leave him away from home for the first time. We had looked forward to seeing him every weekend – this having been one of them.

My sister was away in London at this time. Having left school at eighteen, she then went to Art College, trained as an architect, married and was expecting her first son. Her character was very much like my father's, and as a sister to me she was really quite removed from my world, being so much older, and never actually took much interest in me. She was much quieter than Tim, whose exuberance was abundant. These last three years of my life were to set the pattern of things to come.

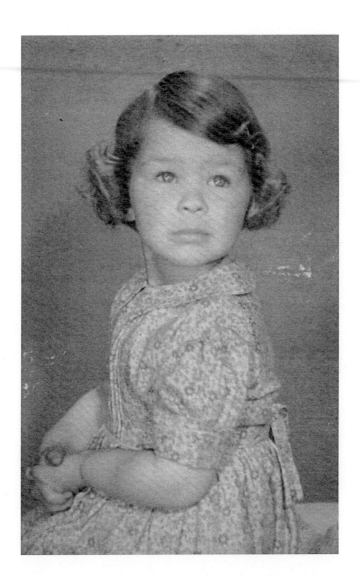

Self at approx 24 months.

'I wonder what's up there?' Minehead beach.

Franklin Leslie and his sisters Laura & Alice playing chess.

My mother, Marjorie Leslie.

My father John (Ron) Grose.

Mother as a 'Vamp'

Happy day!

My father - 'down & out' in Australia.

On the farm.

My brother Tim, 1953.

With my sister and nephew Nigel in the South of France.

My girls. Carrie, Lucy, Emma & Amanda.

With my first grandchild Jamielee.

CHAPTER 3

I was on my way home, with a warm feeling of security creeping over me with each decreasing mile. The rhythm of the old steam train, solid and dependable was beating out the message 'taking me home, taking me home, taking me home'. The familiar rich green countryside flashed past the window, instilling a sense of childlike reassurance, and now and then the odd puff of smoke from the engine interrupted my view. The London city smog was being pushed further and further behind and my life there diminishing with the miles as though it had been a dream. I had been so eager to explore it and so full of expectations. Now it felt a slightly sordid unreality, tinged with a sense of foreboding, yet the lure of it and the promise of glamour, excitement and adventure had been irresistible. How blind one is at seventeen! Whilst I do admit there had been some highlights, on the whole, I was leaving behind the struggle for survival, loneliness in bedsit land, and a slightly broken heart, from an unrequited love affair. Whether his or mine I wasn't sure, but I would undoubtedly get over it!

The happy and sad memories slowly came back to me as the train ate up the miles. The dolls' house my father had made me with roses painted round the door, my kitten and my rabbit. Great crested newts that I had fished out of a pond and put in an old galvanized bath in the garden, and sometimes took for walks on the lawn! On freezing winter days, racing like the wind down a snow-covered hilly field on a toboggan made by my father. It was a beautiful one, painted green with steel runners and was capable of seating three quite comfortably. The field had a large tree stump at the bottom, which obviously everyone did their best to avoid, but if disaster did occur, one could find oneself flying through the air to be dumped unceremoniously in a tangle of brambles, beyond which lay a very murky pond! My brother and his friend making cider in the garage, while I watched, fascinated, as the apples squirted out juice from a home-made press into a bucket. They got heartily sick of my following them around and I was often told, rather crushingly, to 'push off'!

Tim, although being rather a merciless tease, was a very sweet and loving brother to me and, I recall, on one of his school sports days he took my hand and led me round the field explaining all the events and even introducing me to various masters and friends (I fell in love with an African high-jumper called Luke!). Most boys of fifteen would rather have completely disowned a smaller sister at such a public occasion. He even resorted to knitting my dolls' clothes for me, especially one Christmas when I received a complete outfit of hat, dress, knickers and shoes for my new doll! My uncle Alec had taught him to knit when home on leave one year, and he became very good at it. When I was small, I used to crawl into Tim's bed first thing in the morning and he would read me stories before going to school.

The walks in the country with my father on a Sunday morning. The lush green of the Somerset countryside open to us to explore, and trickling streams, which we forded in Wellington boots. We would pick hazelnuts and bluebells, and gather bunches of wild flowers to take home to my mother. Sometimes we would catch the farmers out ferreting, the ferocious little animals scrabbling frantically at a burrow to reach the poor trapped rabbit inside.

> The warmth, the safety of strong arms
> To dissipate those early qualms
> The walks we took, my hand in his
> There was no play to equal this
> Strong, like an ox, of sturdy frame
> How silently he played the game
> A man of few words, full of love
> And like a giant he towered above
> The hand encompassed in his own
> Would never feel it had outgrown
> This haven of paternity.

Going to local 'meets' and following the hunt in our car, the riders in their hunting pink leaping crazily over hedges and ditches, tearing across fields with the bugle 'hallooing' and the hounds yelping excitedly ahead. My father was never happier than in the country, following country pursuits – the country or the sea.

At weekends in summer we packed a picnic and headed for Dunster beach to fish for grey mullet and mackerel with a homemade net. Some of our neighbours would sometimes come along in their cars to help with the circling and pulling in of the net, which would be approximately twenty to thirty yards long, cork floats on top, lead weights along the bottom, one person either end, and two or three people in the middle to keep it up. Sometimes me with my head just clearing the water! My father would lead off in an arc from the beach, gathering the fish, which when the net neared the shore, leapt up frantically in an effort to escape, making the sea a boiling whirlpool of vibrant life. Some of them escaped over the top and one large one, to everyone's great amusement, darted through our neighbour's legs on one occasion, knocking him over! The beach would suddenly come alive with excited people, all eager to help pull in the catch and trying to hold the fish in. My father would put them into a large wicker basket, giving a considerable number away. There were far too many to take home on a good day.

We had a large Talbot car with leather upholstery and built-in picnic tables in the back, which Tim and I thought great fun to use on rainy days. It must have been rather like driving a tank, but it was a beautiful car. When very little, I can remember the mud of Minehead and Watchet oozing up between my toes and hating it, turning round and suddenly realizing how far out I had ventured and waiting in abject misery until someone came to fetch me!

By the side of the road, on the approach to Dunster beach, there was a tumble-down shack built of large boulders and sporting a battered and rusty corrugated iron roof. An old hermit lived there with a very scruffy little dog. Sometimes he would be sitting outside in the sun when we passed, and we would be filled with eager anticipation each time we went, hoping we would see him. One day we arrived to find his home had been completely demolished, and only a pile of loose boulders and the odd tin can remained. It was a very sad day, and we wondered what could have happened to bring about such desecration.

My father had a succession of old cars, and it was always a moment of great excitement when he acquired a new one. In a moment of madness he came home with an MG sports car, very low and none too safe-looking. My mother was not at all impressed. Fate would have it that my sister Jan was getting married in London at that time, and we all had to travel in this vehicle to the wedding, with Tim and myself squeezed into the back. It rained the whole way, dripping through the canvas roof and down the inside of the detachable Perspex window beside my mother. I think it even came through the floor! We were a very soggy sight on arrival. It couldn't have been a worse car to pick for the occasion, and needless to say it did not stay with us for long, my mother refusing to ride in it any more.

My mother's parents, as I have said, lived next door, with her sister Helen looking after them, together with a Scottish nurse who came daily. My grandfather was very frail by this time, and my grandmother none too strong. It was a large corner house with a sweeping garden, and my pre-school years were mostly spent there. My father extracted some planks from the dividing fence so that we could easily come and go. My grandmother used to sit in the drawing-room and crochet, while I took her long black hair pins out of an Indian tortoiseshell and silver container and laboriously threaded them into a cane chair! She appeared very ancient to me of course, as I was so young, being the baby of the family, though I do remember her being very sweet, gentle and kind. It is such a shame that I hadn't really known my grandparents at all. She died when I was only three, my grandfather preceding her.

Helen's kindness, sternness, generosity and understanding I can well remember, including being told not to slide on the hall mat or down the banisters, and not to sniff! She was always there for my mother when needed, and bought my uniform and sports equipment etc. when times were extra hard. In the summer I helped her sow seeds and weed her garden, pick raspberries and strawberries, and all of us played croquet on the lawn. I even had my sandpit in one corner. I spent much more time there than I did at home, but I suppose it must have been quite a welcome relief for my mother not to have me under her feet all the time.

My brother was always up to mischief, frequently performing hair-raising stunts and needed more of her supervision than I did. She used to keep a small cane on top of the kitchen cupboard, as a deterrent when he was older, but whenever she wanted to wave it at him, she could never find it, and Tim would just walk out of the house with a broad grin on his face! He was always cheerful and full of fun. He would tear round on his bicycle and come to a screeching halt, with his legs spread wide, on the gravel outside our kitchen door, leaving track marks about ten feet long, which he thought great fun, but my father got rather annoyed at the condition of the path. He and a friend built a beautiful tree house with a surprisingly sturdy roof and door. They took me up one day as a special treat, and the view from the top was a breath-taking revelation!

Helen adored Tim. She loved his wicked sense of humour and zest for life. Not having married and with no children of her own, she looked upon us as being as much her children as my mother's I think. We certainly got the equivalent in 'tellings off'! My own mother's selfless devotion and love for us all we took for granted. She had tremendous strength of character and showed great courage in the face of what must have been seemingly insurmountable problems; her own comfortable upbringing being but a memory and not equipping her for the harsh reality that being married to my father seemed to create.

My father was always making things. In our garage he would make the most beautiful models of cars with every tiny piece hand-turned on a lathe. Some of his models in those days were exhibited in the New York Trade Fair. He made cupboards, dressing tables and, in fact, anything my mother happened to need. He later went on to make himself a twenty-foot sailing dinghy and a thirty-foot cabin cruiser, after which came beautiful model ships in silver-plated copper and wood, many of which were sold, with my mother prodding from behind!

The memory of our move to Weston-super-Mare came flooding back to me, and the dread I felt at leaving Taunton and the security of the town where I was born. Changing schools, leaving friends and launching into the unfamiliar released a sense of panic and a heavy heart. I intuitively knew the halcyon days were over and that my life was about to take a turn for the worse.

From the very beginning, I considered Weston to be an alien experience, with nothing in it with which I could identify. It was a seasonal town, a ghost town in winter and overrun with visitors in the summer, all clamouring for candy-floss, the pier and the miles of golden sand, not to mention the mud, which people came from miles around to bathe in for its rejuvenating properties. I'm afraid I did not participate in this recreation as I had had an aversion to mud from a very early age!

I started a new school on arrival in which, needless to say, I was not very happy. I seemed only to have to say my name was 'Phillippa' when the taunting started. 'Ooooh – Ph-i-ll-i-ppa' was the reply, and I was then persecuted because of my accent. I was always having to defend myself in some way. Towards the end, I gave up, joined the wrong crowd and rebelled. Boys were becoming involved and I had to fight even harder to keep my head above water. The competition was great and I didn't want to miss out! I developed (when out!) a slight Somerset accent and tried very hard not to be who I was. I don't think I was terribly nice to know at home during this period. Everything my mother had taught me didn't seem to count for much in the 'real world'.

I never felt I really belonged, although I must admit there were some pleasurable moments. My first kiss behind the boathouse was from Brian, a boy I had been passionately in love with from the moment I saw him, having his name written on my desk, pencil box and anything else I could think of to put it on! He was a sea-cadet, tall, strong, good-looking, blonde and very sunburnt, as we all were then. I'm afraid there was always a girlfriend lurking around, and it was only between their splitting up and making up that I ever had a chance, and I never actually got him. I did, however, instruct him in the art of 'French kissing' for which I think he was (and still must be) truly grateful! My own instruction in this art came from the source – a French student!

I had made friends with a girl called Anne, who lived a few houses away from us, and she and I rather attached ourselves to the sea-cadets, their lives being more exciting than those of the other local boys, and we had some happy and adventurous times with them. Sing-songs round a camp fire (some of which I could certainly not repeat and remember blushing over at the time), and on occasion going out in the whaler with them. We got up at four o'clock one morning, and together joined them to go sprat fishing. I had just finished knitting a new jumper and thought this an ideal opportunity to christen it. We had a wonderful trip out, and I arrived home soaking wet and covered in fish scales! I shook off the scales and put my jumper over a fire guard in front of the fire to dry. On checking half an hour later to see how it was getting on, horrors! It had fallen into the fire and lay a smouldering rust-coloured mass, totally irredeemable. Happiness at a price!

Behind the boathouse lay an expanse of tarmac, walled off from the sea with a cliff beyond. On stormy days at high tide we would all congregate there, going up to the edge and, when a wave broke over it, racing back to see if we could escape the wall of water and spray that cascaded over it – not successfully on many occasions.

Anne was rather an odd friend at times. Quite often, if we disagreed about some trivial thing, she would suddenly leave and go home. This happened one summer day when we were climbing the aforementioned cliff. She suddenly said, having reached the top, and that she was going home, and left me at the bottom!

My mother began taking foreign students, which we all rather enjoyed, and although very hard work for her, she enjoyed trying to converse in German and French. I'm not sure how it came about, but I began calling her 'Mutti', and she remained 'Mutti' for a long time. The students were really great fun and very amusing, with everyone gesticulating wildly, trying to make themselves understood in various languages: Icelandic, Swedish, German and French. There seemed to be two types of French girl – one with rather greasy and spotty skin, always administering 'ampoules' of liquid vitamins and minerals and swallowing a variety of pills (for good health), and definitely leaning towards hypochondria; and the other of definite stronger substance, being chic, self-assured, gamine and beautiful with what would seem to be an aura of a secret knowledge of the world and men, and a naturally superior tolerance of the same! (1 think perhaps that I have secretly adopted the latter approach to a certain degree!) I learnt how to apply make-up and was given tips on Parisian chic from one particular rather lovely French student called Adele.

At school I had started writing to a French boy, Jean-Claude, as a pen-pal, and he decided he would like to come to England, which he did two summers running. We kept up quite a serious relationship, becoming an 'item' as they say. I suppose, on looking back, he was quite patient with me, as everyone else seemed to be sleeping around in those days, except me – it being on the brink of the swinging Sixties and free love being the norm. However, I would not give in! On my leaving for Italy with Jan and her children one summer for a holiday, and his departure for his home in Antibes, we vowed to keep in touch. I did, in fact, see him again when I was in Richmond, but he had changed so much that I wondered what I had ever seen in him.

Having to entertain the students we had staying with us, we arranged barbecues on the beach, riding trips and tennis matches and dancing in the evenings at the local disco. I loved dancing, and this was the highlight of their stays with us as far as I was concerned.

When out on one of the riding excursions one day, we were

cantering through a wood, when my mount decided to completely ignore my efforts to control it and began galloping crazily after the horses in front. One stirrup went flying into the undergrowth never to be seen again, and I clung on grimly to its rather short mane, trying in vain to assert some authority over the animal, and silently praying someone would turn round and see me in this uncontrollable abandonment and come to my rescue. No sooner had my prayers been completed than my head struck an overhead branch and my hard hat was whipped off and hung suspended down my back by the attached elastic, which then proceeded to slowly strangle me for the ensuing few minutes.

Eventually someone realized that I was no longer with them and that my thundering hooves were getting fainter! The turn of a curious head in my direction, and rescue was at hand. The horse, realizing the presence of another coming towards it, came to an erratic and juddering halt. My bone-shattering escapade was over and comparative calm prevailed. Nevertheless, I was considerably shaken in more ways than one, and I have never quite regained the affinity with horses that I thought I once had!

When I was a bit older, the students became more studious and I spent less time with them and more time with Anne and what we referred to as the 'Knightstone' crowd. These were the boys and girls who dived and swam off the slipway near the Knightstone Theatre, some belonging to the nearby Yacht Club, the fishermen and the trip-boat owners, and the boys who ran the Marine Lake. My father also moored his sailing dinghy there, and although I know I must have disappointed him, I did not go out in it very often, not feeling really at home on the sea. This was unlike my sister, who seemed born to it, and was then living with her husband on a Dutch barge on the Thames, having experienced a good deal of sailing in Torquay beforehand.

I had admired Mike from a distance. Being older than the rest he had an air of experience about him and was good-looking in a Steve McQueen sort of way, and always messing about with girls, prodding them with a boat hook or, alternatively, coming to their rescue if they were stuck without a paddle (which a number of girls engineered on purpose – including me). He was in charge of the hired rowing boats at the lake in the summer, and Anne and I spent our holidays there, either rowing or sunbathing.

I had obviously been somewhat of a frustrating enigma to him, as one evening, after everyone had left, I found myself, possibly by design on my part, talking to him by the open doors of his van. To my shock, I was forced into the van and raped, being told that it was about time I knew the facts of life, and that I'd thank him in the end. I put up quite a fight, but the sheer strength and the weight of him were too much for me. Having held out this long, resisting all who'd gone before, I was terrified at this frightening assault from someone whom I had not only admired but wanted. This feeling of powerlessness has dogged me throughout my life, this lack of being in control, and yet to outward appearances I am in complete control, perhaps to the point of seeming rather aloof.

I climbed shakily onto my bike and rode home. It was very late and I hoped desperately that my parents would not be up to see me. They were not, and I went straight to bed, feeling dirty, bitterly ashamed and humiliated, and telling no one. I was fifteen. This, and my previous experiences, did nothing to enhance my opinion of men. I think it even affected my relationship with my own father, in that I unconsciously kept him at a distance. I hope for his sake he didn't notice. No one ever spoke of any of the past encounters I had had, and I had learnt from an early age to hide my feelings. I lived with the guilty feeling of being different from my friends, and having a secret to hide. I didn't tell my mother in this instance, because I really didn't think she'd understand or be able to help – I also felt I had done something wrong. My mother also knew Mike. He had been an ambulance driver, and had come to the house to pick up one of our students when she had broken her leg. She said how nice and helpful he had been, so I thought perhaps she might not even believe me.

This was the beginning of the age of the Teddy Boys, and Anne and I frequented the amusement arcades, listening to the juke boxes and playing the fruit machines. The gangs used to hang out there, causing great excitement when a fight broke out – though this in fact was very frightening. The Bristol Teddy Boys used to come to Weston on the train at the weekend, and especially on bank holidays, walking five or six abreast, as in a Wild West film, down the main street, sporting knuckle dusters and swinging bicycle chains, for the sole purpose of fighting our local boys. They wore Edwardian-style, knee-length skirted coats called 'drapes', with cuffs either of velvet or satin, with several pockets. They had narrow drainpipe trousers, brocade waistcoats, stiff shirts and shoestring, bootlace or 'Slim Jim' ties, finished off with crepe-soled suede shoes called 'brothel creepers'. Their hair was slicked back into a wavy, quiff style with long sideburns, the back being styled into a D.A. (duck's arse) by running a comb down the centre. The atmosphere would be electric with the threat of a possible clash of these Titans! The Weston boys, led by Billy Marshall and Pete Fry, two equally menacing and powerful-looking opponents, would meet these gangs head-on, similarly equipped with weapons of bloodthirsty and barbaric nature.

Anne and I, definitely not a part of this, would stand on the side-lines and watch the action, being rather careful not to be seen to be involved with the girlfriends of these boys, as it could quite possibly end in disaster, though we did in fact know Frieda, Pete Fry's girl. Before very long a fight would break out, sirens would wail and the Black Mariah (large black van with double doors at the rear and benches either side of the interior) would arrive to cart them all off to the local police station where they would be relieved of their weapons and given a 'bed for the night'! Fun over, we would go back to our records and fruit machines! The girls in those days, the late 1950s and early 1960s, were not quite so extreme in their dress, though we had a definite style of our own. I remember making circle skirts, which were worn with layers and layers of net petticoats underneath, flying out around us when we jived (showing a good deal of leg and knicker), as did our hair which was tied back in ponytails.

CHAPTER 4

Leaving school was a blessed release for me. They were certainly not the happiest days of my life, being more of a practical and artistic person than academic, and at last I was able to please myself, or so I thought, but my mother had other ideas. I was coerced into going to secretarial college, when really I should have liked to have studied art and the piano! My sister had done both, and I was always rather envious. However, the secretarial training stood me in good stead for many years, and I was never unemployed for any length of time, as secretaries were always in demand. The college was run by two spinster sisters (I seem to attract them) Dolly and Daisy Pearce, and the only thing that I can with accuracy remember is that every morning Dolly would come into the room bearing Daisy's daily intake of Lucozade! We students all thought it rather funny and odd. Daisy herself was a good teacher, however, and got us all through the necessary exams to take us on into the world of business.

My first job was in an estate agent's in Weston, which I didn't find terribly interesting, and the people were rather dull. I then went on to Transport House in Bristol, travelling up and back by train. I used to enjoy the journey back in winter best. There were about half a dozen Transport House employees bound in the same direction, and we formed a small group. One of the guys played the guitar well, and we used to sing our way happily home! Those old carriages had a beautiful cosy feeling, with the train rattling through the cold and darkness, and us all snug and warm singing inside!

I was sixteen and working in Bristol when I met Chuck. He was tall, with curly blond hair and looked very handsome in his RAF uniform, and was stationed at the RAF base at Yeovil. He was a lovely guy, and we had a serious relationship for several months until I woke up one fateful morning thinking I might be pregnant. I kept it to myself, not daring to tell my parents. I had very sweet letters from Chuck on expensive light coffee coloured notepaper in really beautiful black-inked copper-plate writing, telling me not to worry, and that everything was going to be all right. Unfortunately, it wasn't! Days went by and I became quite distraught about it, eventually having to tell my mother. A grave mistake. I had never seen my mother so out of control. She literally shouted and screamed at me and with shaking hands found and tore up all my beautiful letters from Chuck, and I was forbidden to see him again. All this for a false alarm! I was out one evening a few weeks later with a friend and almost bumped into him. He turned and was about to speak to me when my so-called friend pulled at my arm, saying 'You don't want to bother with him!', and literally dragged me away. I wonder to this day what he was going to say.

My relationship with my parents broke down completely and I could not forgive my mother for her lack of understanding. Of course she could not have known that my innocence had been violated several months before, and that Chuck had nothing to do with the sullying of her daughter. In fact he had treated me with the utmost chivalry. This would have been an ideal time to tell her about what had happened to me earlier with Mike, but I never even thought of doing so. My father never seemed to enter into it, leaving the general chastisement to my mother, which looking back wasn't exactly fair. Her lack of knowledge and understanding of the world surrounding her daughter obviously did not help the situation at all. However, I cannot actually blame her for not knowing how to deal with events that were totally alien to her, though it would have made such a difference if I had had a comforting arm around me and a degree of sympathy, but I'm afraid nothing like that ever came my way. To show any outward demonstration of affection was not 'the done thing' in both my mother's and my father's backgrounds. Stiff upper lip at all times!

From then on we barely exchanged a civil word and I made up my mind to leave home. Bristol was not exciting enough to hold me, and I found myself drawn to London. My parents were very alarmed at the idea of my going alone to such a vice-ridden city, and were vehemently against it. So much so, and so determined was I, that I'm afraid to say I packed my suitcase and was about to leave, whether they liked it or not. Fortunately, they found the suitcase and halted my departure, but obviously realized I was serious in my intentions.

Arrangements were made, and I went up to Twickenham to stay with Jan. She and her husband were still living on the Dutch barge at the time, which I very much enjoyed. To wake up to the sound of the water lapping against the hull, and to see the morning sun through the portholes glinting on the water, was lovely. However, it wasn't very warm in the winter! My brother-in-law was not exactly a dab-hand at renovations. Everything on the boat was make-shift. I remember the loo was just curtained off and extremely embarrassing to use! It was the same with the washing facilities.

My brother-in-law gave up his 'converting' in the end and we all moved quite soon into a house on the towpath opposite, which was shaped rather like a tram, with big bay windows front and back. It also had a flat roof the length of the house, which Jan and I used for sunbathing (in the buff) and we used to wave to the planes that passed overhead on their way to and from Heathrow! I think perhaps the pilots had other things on their minds than ogling two nude ladies waving frantically at them! The boat people were a lively and interesting crowd, some rather 'arty' types to whom I found I was rather drawn, such as writers and cameramen working in television and films.

The Dutch barge *Leiden* was eventually sold to a young couple in their thirties who set about transforming her into a luxury boat for charter in the Mediterranean. Her brass fittings were polished, her decks caulked, cabins with double bunks built, a spanking new galley, luxury shower and loo installed. Having been a very tired, sad and dishevelled old lady, she rose proud and gleaming and ready to embark on hitherto unexplored destinations with a shining new lease of life. Numerous parties took place on board the boat, with interesting and exciting people attending – writers, actors and musicians. I met Gordon, a cameraman, at one of them and went out with him for quite a while. He had a basement flat on Richmond Hill, in the bathroom of which hung a shrunken head, which was rather disconcerting! He also had a boat whose bottom he was scraping in the boatyard in Duck's Walk, and I used to help him work on it occasionally. I gave him up eventually, as behind the camera he turned out to be rather too serious.

I had another brief encounter with Richard Harris (scriptwriter of *A Touch of Frost*, *Sherlock Holmes* etc.), who I went out with a few times, though found that we really didn't 'connect', by which I mean that we didn't have much to say to each other! He had a houseboat in Cubitt's Basin, which was quite fun. I had also met him at a party on the Dutch barge. (Much later I contacted him with regard to the screenplay for a television production of this book. With my inevitable 'luck' he was on the point of retiring from writing for television, though did say he thought it good enough for production, but it needed a 'hook', something like a murder to hang the story on.)

I found a job in Richmond without too much trouble, with a firm of estate agents. Being very junior, my boss decided to call me Pip-squeak, and I seemed to fit in very well, enjoying the rather fatherly attention he gave me and the friendly atmosphere of the office. Finding I could talk to people easily, I enjoyed working as a receptionist and telephonist more than the actual clerical side of things. I made a very good friend there, Audrey, who, being about ten years older, was wiser than I and proved a good confidante and buffer for my troubles.

I went through a rather odd phase of being a semi Beatnik, and dressed in long black/charcoal sweaters over skin-tight pencil skirts or drainpipe jeans, my eyes being made up with black kohl eye liner, black mascara and very pale pink lipstick (not for the office though). The hair was worn in a French pleat or a beehive, or both!

I contacted a rather odd Beatnik friend called Tony whom I had known in Weston (we used to sit around reading and listening to poetry) as I knew he lived in London, and we met up for evenings out sometimes. He took me to places such as the Station Hotel, L'Auberge and Eel Pie Island, where I learnt a dance called the Stomp! This dance, with several couples doing it, made the floor literally bounce up and down. Eel Pie Island, a hotel on an island in the Thames near Richmond, was known for its amazing bands, playing Blues and Trad Jazz in the 1960s. Rather shifty looking characters went there, a selection of whom could always be found smoking spliffs sitting on the river bank, and everything in their lives was 'way out man'! I fortunately did not smoke in those days, and these rather pathetic souls I considered to be rather beneath me and far too serious! I was very much an onlooker during this period, and watched it all with fascination from the sidelines. Very famous names started in these clubs, such as Eric

Clapton, Jeff Beck, Rod Stewart and, of course, the Rolling Stones.

Coming home from work each night in the winter could be rather frightening at times. We seemed to get much more fog in those days than I've encountered of late. Anyhow, coming across Richmond Bridge and turning off along the towpath known as Duck's Walk, which ran along by the river, when you could hardly see your hand in front of your face, was very unnerving. The fog was much thicker here and hung like an impenetrable wet blanket. I was walking my usual route from work in the fog one evening just after five, and had got about half-way along the towpath I suppose, when a man in a raincoat, pushing a bicycle, loomed up in front of me and as he passed his arm came out and grabbed me. I could feel his clenched hand on me, and then he just moved on. I went hot and cold all over with revulsion and fear, and quickened my pace, in fact ended up running the last fifty yards or so to safety and home. I felt very odd when I got home, thinking perhaps that I'd dreamt it, the fog conjuring up an eerie feeling of detachment from reality, but I'm sure I hadn't!

I went from the estate agency to work at London University for a time, which was incredibly boring, being stuck in a back room all the time, typing out mountains of theses for students. I lasted only a few weeks there before giving in my notice, in search of pastures new.

I had met a chap who was setting up in business, making films for visual juke boxes (an early form of videos I suppose). I went to work for him for a short while in an office in Gray's Inn

Road in London. Although I wasn't there very long (there wasn't enough money to keep the company going) I did have quite an interesting time, attending auditions and doing recordings in Shepperton Studios with the pop bands of the time, only two of which I can remember with any clarity. Those were Paul and Paula and the French singer Françoise Hardy. Kenneth More and Dirk Bogarde were there at the time, though each acting in different films; Kenneth More in *The Comedy Man* and Dirk Bogarde in *The Life of Franz Liszt*. I passed Kenneth More several times in the corridor, smiling a 'Hello'.

The boys played a trick on me while we were there. Knowing I secretly wanted to meet Dirk Bogarde they explained that he was doing a scene playing the piano in the studio next door for the biographical film of Franz Liszt, and that they had arranged for me to meet him. I was dreadfully nervous but terribly excited. As I entered the studio I was greeted with the wonderful music of Franz Liszt being played by a man seated at the piano with his back to me, and as I approached Mike started to introduce me. The man in question turned round and stood up. He was only about five feet six tall, but he almost had the face of Dirk Bogarde – he was in fact a remarkably similar double. You can imagine that I was slightly disappointed! However, I did see the real Dirk Bogarde quite often in the canteen and had to be content with that.

When this job came to an end, I rang up BBC Television and asked them if they had any vacancies. Luckily they had (it was so much easier to get into the BBC then) and after a successful interview, I started work in the Sound Department of Light Entertainment as secretary to the Sound Supervisor. I found television quite fascinating, and the people I worked with were an interesting and friendly crowd. Many well-known faces would come and go during a day's work. On one of my reconnoitres of the studios, I happened to look in on *Top of the Pops*, and sitting on one of the tiered benches, I was approached by Adam Faith. He began talking to me and asked me for a date. Like an idiot I said 'I don't think so thank you!' I really can't imagine why, except that he wore the most awful royal blue sequinned jacket!

Another reconnoitre of Studio 3 put me in touch with Kenneth More again and Michael Bentine! Both had obviously had a liquid lunch and were supposed to be recording a programme on some sort of wildlife as they seemed to have a tank of tropical fish in front of them. However, it was not going terribly well, as they kept giggling! Kenneth More came to sit beside me, and rather cheekily I asked 'Do you remember me? We met at Shepperton Studios'. His reply was to get off the chair, kneel down and kiss my knee! He then said, 'How charming. I'm sure if we had met I should have remembered you'. I wasn't quite sure how to take that, and was certainly loath to wash that knee!

The Sound Department supervises the sound crews, their microphones etc., and the planning and allocation of each crew to a programme. I teamed up with another girl there and joined SADG (Studio Amateur Dramatic Group) and she and I went over to Broadcasting House once a week to try our hands at acting. One week we had to imagine we were trapped in the cockpit of a stricken aircraft, dropping into the sea. I screamed my head off and she banged and crashed about, trying to portray panic and terror! We put absolutely everything we could muster into our performance and I thought we were brilliant. When the director played back the tape there was not one scream of mine or a bang of hers to be heard! They had dubbed someone else's efforts over our own. We were, needless to say, extremely put out! I decided that acting was not for me, as I was so nervous when I had to speak, and my legs shook so, that I did not think it was worth the agony! I don't think it was my friend Anne's forte either, and so we decided to call it a day.

One of my other friends there was Fran, a lovely, kindly middle-aged woman whom I found very easy to talk to. She was telling me how proud she was of her son having just got his pilot's licence. I was immediately fascinated and asking all sorts of questions as to where he flew etc., how long he'd been flying, but most of all, 'Please would he take me up?' Of course she explained that he hadn't been flying very long and had only just obtained his licence etc., and made all sorts of excuses for my not going, but I won in the end! I really can't remember how I actually met up with Michael, or how I got to Biggin Hill; the only thing I can remember is the *flying*! I had always longed to fly in a small plane – and this was it.

The plane was a two-seater Auster and looked quite tiny. However, I climbed on board and Michael strapped me in tightly. He was a tall, good-looking guy and obviously mad about flying, and not very interested in girls! I judged him to be a responsible person and although I had never met him before felt quite safe in his capable hands, and because he was Fran's son I knew that I could trust him with my life. I was not in the least afraid, in fact I felt almost sick with excitement and anticipation of what was to come. Michael started the engine and the little plane began to shudder and vibrate, the propeller's rotations becoming a blur, and we taxied slowly on to the runway. The sound of the engine was now deafening as we came to a halt before take-off. We harnessed more power and with a thundering roar sped down the runway and up into the air. The feel of being pushed down in my seat, the roar of the engine and the rise into the air was fantastic. We soared up into a cloudless azure sky, the ground below getting smaller and smaller until all the fields and houses could have fitted into a sketchbook. He suddenly said 'Hold tight!' and pulling back on the joy-stick the nose of the plane rose up, higher and higher and ultimately over into a roll! I felt as though I were being pushed right through the belly of the plane. He shouted 'We haven't finished yet! with a smile, and then we were off again, but this time doing a spin. The nose of the plane went down and the tail went up – and I lost my grip on the world! This was truly amazing and I saw the countryside spinning round and round like the inside of a washing machine, until we swooped out of it and away. This was a thrill I shall never forget, and before I leave this world I want to learn to *fly*!

Thank you so much Michael for a truly heavenly experience.

Of course the history of Biggin Hill is very important, having played a major part in World War Two. There are squadrons in the RAF as proud at having fought from there as regiments in the army are of having 'Blenheim' and 'Alamein' emblazoned on their colours. To stand on this hallowed ground and survey the vast expanse of runway, and the buildings that had been instrumental in orchestrating the lives of airmen in the past, was really humbling and quite awesome. To think that brave young men had climbed into their planes, perhaps for the first time after their inadequate few weeks' training, feeling sick with fright at what was to come, some of them not returning, was an extremely sobering thought. Others perhaps returning from a sortie to find their comrades gone, dossing down for a few hours' sleep then up again into a sky full of terror, knowing all too well that they might be the next on the list. After my flight I stood rather pensively on the runway thinking of those brave young men, also the young women who ferried the planes the width and breadth of the country, and the families left behind in a void of hopelessness and sorrow.

Some buildings are modern, while others bear the scars of war, patches of raw brickwork and the fading patterns of camouflage. Its history lies in the dusty files and combat reports, and in the treasured diaries and memories of the men and women who have served there. However, the Kent Flying Club celebrated their arrival at Biggin Hill in 1959 and its days as a civil operated aerodrome began, the memories of bygone battles fading into the distance.

CHAPTER 5

With my changing jobs inevitably came a change of residences, and bedsit land began in earnest. I moved from Jan's into a bedsit in Richmond, then on to Hammersmith and finally Chiswick. Apart from my work, I found life very lonely, and nowhere near as thrilling as I had hoped. However, there was one bright spot in all the gloom! I cannot let my time in London go by without mentioning Brian. He was a lovely man. Sadly, I was not attracted to him physically, his being about forty to my eighteen, but he possessed a wonderful sense of humour and fun, and treated me like a queen. I met him at a party, and from then on seemed to spend most of my dates with him. He was high up in the classical music world of conducting, and was then Music Director of the Royal Shakespeare Theatre at Stratford-on-Avon (where I went with him to sit through some rather painful auditions of children dancing and singing! Lunch in the 'Dirty Duck' pub after – this pub is officially known as the 'White Swan', though is affectionately referred to as the 'Dirty Duck' by locals and actors alike).

He has since travelled all over the world, from University of

Cape Town, University of Kansas, Stockholm Conservatoire, Brussels Conservatoire and Mexico City teaching graduate courses in conducting. He was also Music Director and Conductor of the Denver Orchestra. He introduced operas in English for the first time and appeared on television with the BBC and also ABC. A brilliant, compassionate and lovely man. He frequently visited different theatres etc. and would take me backstage to meet the cast of whatever play was on. After the show at the Globe Theatre one evening we looked in on Christopher Plummer in his dressing room, the latter sporting a very fetching pair of black tights and nothing else! He had just come off stage having been playing the lead in Richard III.

After Brian had introduced us we arranged to meet up for dinner at The Village (a restaurant in, if I remember rightly, St John's Wood). Copious amounts of wine flowed that evening, being passed up and down a very long trestle-type table, at which sat Dorothy Tutin, Sir John Gielgud, Patrick Wymark, Maggie Smith, Chris Plummer, Brian and myself, plus several other actors whose names I can't remember, or actually perhaps never knew. I ended the evening playing the piano and singing 'Bye, Bye Blackbird' alongside Chris Plummer, both of us definitely the worse for wear!

I was wined and dined by Brian at some lovely restaurants and hotels, the Hilton, Les Ambassadeurs, Quaglinos, the Dorchester, Inn on the Park and many other smaller Italian and Chinese restaurants that he knew, and the parties we went to were always frequented by fascinating people, actors, musicians and writers etc. I remember meeting John Leyton (of the film *The Great Escape*) at one of them, and rather fancied him! When taking me to see the stage production of *West Side Story*, we met up with Sir John Gielgud at the bar in the interval. I found him to be a very dour man, not much humour there, unless terribly 'dry'!

I always felt special when I was out with Brian, and many times was serenaded in our favourite spot, the Trattoria in Soho. They knew Brian well, and as we went there often they got to know me too, which was a nice feeling. This, I thought, was what London was all about and what I had expected and hoped it would be. After a few weeks of seeing a good deal of Brian he asked me if I would consider going with him on holiday to the South of France. It was rather difficult, as I didn't want to hurt his feelings and I desperately wanted to go. In the end I told him I would love to, but on my terms. Nothing physical! He went home and mulled this over, and after a few days I received a postcard 'Come with me on YOUR TERMS!' So I packed my bags and we were off.

We flew by charter flight in a rather battered DC10, which rattled its way from Lydd to Orly Airport in Paris, our intention being to stay in the city for a couple of days. Brian's car had been delivered to the airport, a Triumph convertible that, with the top down, my long hair blowing in the wind as we raced along under the scorching sun, evoked a wonderful feeling of freedom on the open road!

Paris was wonderful. I had never been before and we arrived

the day before the 14th July celebrations. Brian took me to the top of the Eiffel Tower (incidentally it does sway!) and, looking down, the whole of Paris lay before me in an intricate pattern of greys and greens, the roads appearing like hairline cracks, and the River Seine running through it reflecting the sky, a ribbon of blue.

The preparations for the 14th July were well under way – flags flying everywhere, and banners and bunting being attached to every lamp-post and tree. By about eight o'clock the following evening the city was a seething mass of jostling humanity, all trying to get as close to the river and the Pont Neuf (new bridge) as possible, where the firework display was to take place. This was the most amazing explosion of noise and colour I have ever seen, lighting up Paris for miles around. The city went mad with people drunkenly singing and dancing well into the next day.

We left the next morning in a slightly hung-over state, for Lyon and our subsequent journey to the coast. We passed through St Etienne and the beautiful Loire Valley, then down to Nimes, Arles and then across the Camargue, which had an air about it of having been forgotten. Wild stretches of salt marshes and lagoons, completely naked of trees, with amazingly abundant bird life such as herons, cormorants, eagles and flamingos, and of course white horses and the famous black bulls, on which the herons perched precariously.

The bulls are rounded up once a year and driven through the narrow streets of Arles for the ensuing bull-fights.

Incidentally the bulls are never killed in a *course camarguaise*, as can happen in the Spanish *corrida*. The native white horses and large black bulls and their entourage roam quite freely on the land, as they have probably done since prehistoric times, grazing on the marram grass that edges the swamps.

We ran into a swarm of rather large flying insects, which dive-bombed the windscreen of the car, splattering it horribly until it was impossible to see where we were going. Not a pleasant experience, as I have a horror of small flying objects, and these were particularly nasty, being *en masse*. We had to frantically haul up the roof and shut the windows tightly, with a mass of insects swarming around our heads! Having achieved this we then found ourselves imprisoned until the threatening cloud decided that we were not perhaps as interesting as they had first thought. To my horror, a couple of them had been trapped inside whilst we were putting up the roof and, although I'm normally reasonably brave, I curled up into a terrified ball under the glove compartment, leaving Brian to get rid of them!

We visited Saintes-Maries-de-la-Mer, where a gypsy festival is held each year. Legend has it that Mary Salome, mother of the apostles James and John, and Mary Jacob, the sister of the Virgin Mary, fled Palestine by boat along with their Ethiopian servant Sarah and several other disciples and landed on these shores, and it is said that this town was the first place in Camargue to adopt the Christian faith. All the disciples on the boat continued on by foot, venturing deeper into the

Camargue preaching their gospels and bringing faith to the Gauls, except the two Marys who remained behind and built an altar in Saintes-de-la-Mer where the present church now stands. The servant Sarah is revered by gypsies, her status having been raised to Saint Sarah, patron saint of gypsies and travellers. The bones of the two Saint Marys are incarcerated in a wooden chest, which, each year, during the festival, are transported down the beach flanked by guardians on white horses, into the Mediterranean Sea, amidst a cacophony of wailing prayers and protestations! However, we were not able to see this wonderful spectacle, as it was the wrong time of year.

Eventually we said goodbye to the Camargue and its barren landscape and headed along the coast road to Nice, our destination being St Paul de Vence, a tiny village up in the hills behind. This road had rather alarming hairpin bends and an equally terrifying sheer drop on one side, falling away to jagged rocks and scrubland below, with only a very low wall forming a barrier against flying over the edge to early extinction!

I could have stayed in St Paul for ever! It was beautiful, with its tiny cobbled streets and tall shuttered houses, blocking out the sun, with lines of washing hung between them. Brian had a studio apartment at the top of a cobbled hill, which we climbed in the mid-day heat, on up past a pretty old stone well to the end of the street. Waking up in the morning to the smell of ground coffee and freshly baked bread, and the feel of lazy happiness about the place, was heavenly.

I stretched this blissful holiday out as long as I possibly

could, lying in the sun on the edge of the sea, the only cool place to be, and with poor Brian, I'm afraid, not too happy sitting under an umbrella, as he was fair skinned, watching from a distance. We spent our days either on the beach in Nice, walking round the town sightseeing or going for drives in the surrounding beautiful countryside. We also visited a vineyard nearby and sat in the sun sampling the produce and discussing its merits with the owner, a friend of Brian's. Our evenings were quite often spent having dinner in the lovely Colombe d'Or restaurant in St Paul and chatting to the locals there.

I stuck to my guns over 'my terms', although I think he had imagined once there that I would not! Although he was wonderful company and a dear friend, I would not succumb, and he became rather annoyed with me after about a week, and I was eventually put on Le Train Bleu and sent home, much to my chagrin, as I had really loved it all, and apart from this 'thing' between us, we had got on extremely well, and I knew he was fond of me. It was just a pity I couldn't feel the same way. I'm sorry to say that I never saw him again after that – though years later he was still asking after me, I discovered. A great shame, as he was the nicest, most caring man I have ever met. Undoubtedly an opportunity missed!

On my return to London I picked up the threads of an old romance. I had marriage in mind and he had not, so I packed my bags once again, and this time headed for home. I had exhausted London, or perhaps it was the other way around.

I pushed all thoughts of the city out of my mind and sank

back into the cosy upholstery of the compartment to await my arrival at Weston, memories of a complex past stamped out as if by a giant footstep. This was another turning point in my life, and I vaguely wondered what lay ahead. I looked out of the window at the fields and farmhouses flying by and realized that I really didn't care – I was going home.

The train pulled slowly into the station, and I started to collect my things, my suitcase from the rack above me, hoping there would be someone around to carry it, and my various other bits and pieces. These were the days when porters lined the platform, politely tugged the peaks of their caps, called you 'Miss' or 'Madam' and carried your bags for a sixpenny tip. Not so now I fear!

On my arrival in Weston, I found that none of my friends were around any more, and that I was totally out of touch. For want of things to do, my mother persuaded me to join the Young Conservatives. They all decided to have an outing one evening, and we went for a walk to visit the Lifeboat House, after which, on to a local pub for a drink – where I met Mark. I was attracted to him immediately. Good looks, personality and charm! He had chiselled features very similar to those of Stewart Granger. I found him very interesting to talk to, as he had travelled considerably, and coming from an army background, had been on the move most of his life. It was a mutual attraction, and we spent much of our time together.

He started buying quite a number of expensive things, such as sports equipment, cameras and clothes, and I thought to myself that he must have quite a bit of money! Before very long, he asked me to marry him, and I accepted. He bought my engagement ring in a local jeweller's, and I was really very happy – that is until there was a knock on my parents' door one day, and two plain-clothes detectives stood there. All the things he had bought, including my engagement ring, had been acquired with bounced cheques! Mark spent the night in jail, my father put up the bail money, and he was released the next day. Of course, everything he had bought went back to the various shops, but rather than let my ring go, I paid for it myself. This set the scene for a very interesting future. I should have broken off the engagement, of course, but I was foolish enough to be in love! My parents, naturally, were desperately worried about this turn of events, but couldn't sway me from still wanting to marry him.

We decided to move back to London, and rented a bedsit off Cromwell Road. Mark managed to obtain a job chauffeuring, while I went back to a job vacancy I had known about in Richmond with a book company. Before very long, I discovered I was pregnant. Mark's reaction to this was to totally ignore it as though it weren't happening. His court case was imminent and he was terrified. In the meantime, I had a pregnancy to cope with, and the thought of telling my parents made me sick with worry. Although this was the 1960s, with a fair amount of promiscuity around, I knew they would be very upset, and didn't really know what reaction I would get. However, although they were shocked, they stood by me and, by special request, we were married in church in Weston, the vicar being very kind and understanding of my circumstances.

Mark's parents were then living in Windsor and offered to put us up. It seemed the sensible thing to do with more work around in the London area for Mark, and of course there was the anonymity of it. With Weston being a small town, I think perhaps my mother would have been rather ashamed of me! They were just as shocked as my parents had been, but were very good about it and took us in without question, though not before Mark's father had enquired as to whether I was sure that the baby was Mark's! You can imagine my anger and indignation at this.

I wanted desperately to have my baby at home, but it was out of the question, the house being on four floors, and just too many stairs for everyone to cope with in such a situation.

The house backed on to the Long Walk leading up to Windsor Castle, and we would often see one or other member of the Royal family driving past. I did in actual fact hold up the Queen once while pushing Mandy in her pram up the Long Walk! I was quite oblivious of the fact until Mark dragged me to one side, and she swept silently past me, within inches, and I noticed what beautiful skin she had!

My doctor informed me, quite wrongly, that unless I were forty and having my first, I would not be admitted to hospital. We were in a slight quandary. I obviously had to go somewhere, and after some deliberation, a private maternity home was booked. This was run by nuns, who busily swished along the corridors in their habits, had never experienced actually having babies and whom I found very unsympathetic to my condition! I was totally miserable there, being put in a room on my own, and having to ring a bell five times if I wanted anything. This extraordinary bell-ringing ritual had uncannily occurred with my own birth in a private nursing home when my mother gave birth to me! Apparently she too had to ring a bell five times to summon someone, and did so when she thought I was about to appear, and when eventually someone did come, she was offered watercress sandwiches!

After my efforts at summoning one of the nuns, a Sister Fatima rushed down the corridor towards me, and on inspection assured me, in an Irish accent, that I had 'hours to go'. Consequently, my baby was almost born before anyone came near me: Amanda was born at ten to three in the afternoon, arriving with no time to get to the delivery room, and immediately whisked away to be cleaned up, and I did not see her until much later. I knew I had had a girl, but whether she was all right or not no-one would say. They brought her to me several hours later for her first feed, and she was beautiful!

If I could teach you all I know
To save the pain in store
The future I would give to you
No heartaches any more
Our lives are ruled by destiny
Manoeuvre as we may

So trauma is a part of life
And has its role to play
My hands are tied in helplessness
My heart in anguish yearns
To ease the burdens life predicts
Erase the twists and turns
But I can only stand and watch
While fate dictates her plan
Impart the wisdom I have gained
Encompassed in the span
So hold your head up high my child
And walk on through the storm
Remember I have gone before
A smoother path to form

Having had a lovely baby girl, I should have been happy, but in the home no-one seemed to have the time to care. I only saw her at feeding times and as deep snow lay outside, hardly saw Mark at all, as he had to travel from Windsor to Beaconsfield, and very often it was impossible to get through. However, I survived and returned to Windsor nine days after Mandy was born (having begged to come out a day early), with no complications – though the maternity home was never paid! I cannot say I felt terribly guilty about this, as I really didn't think they deserved to be.

Mark was a very loving and generous person, and a good father. This generosity was very often the cause of argument.

He was also a terrible flirt, but then so was I! When we went to parties we would split up and go our separate ways, coming together now and then to see that the other was all right and then parting again! We knew we could trust each other, which I suppose is a rare commodity these days. Life with him was good and I loved him, being an easy person to live with and fun. However, there was always the underlying feeling of insecurity, as I never knew what was going to happen next or where we would be living in only a matter of weeks' time. We had a beautiful little cottage in Farnham once, with a garden full of roses. It was just what I had always wanted, and I thought we were settled, but even taking in a lodger the rent went unpaid and eventually we had to leave. Unfortunately, it was the 'done thing' to leave money matters to the husband in those days, so I had absolutely no control over our finances and trusted Mark to take care of that side of things.

We rented part of a house in Old Windsor temporarily, but found that with a small baby it was not large enough to accommodate all the paraphernalia that came with her. Mark had a South African friend called Eric, living in a large flat in Windsor, with whom we shared for a time. Eric also had a live-in lesbian girlfriend, whom he was desperately trying to convert into being straight! I can't remember her name, but I can still hear in my head the record *A Groovy Kind of Love* being played over and over again, as she was completely obsessed with it! Rather ironic when you think about it.

We were idly chatting about the state of things in England,

when Eric mentioned South Africa and how easy life was out there, how beautiful the climate and why didn't we go back with him? I must say, we did think South Africa a bit far, and our thoughts turned briefly to the South of France instead. Eric was very persuasive though, and we discovered that it would only cost £10 to get us there on an emigration scheme. Since I was very young and reading wonderfully exciting stories by Laurens van der Post and others, I had been drawn to Africa, yearned and dreamed of going there – a dream I thought would never come true, but here we were, on the brink!

Within ten days our passports were obtained, inoculations undergone and Mandy, Mark and I were ready to emigrate. The person taking care of all this was none other than a Russian prince (probably rather hard to believe but nevertheless true). He wore a jade signet ring on his finger bearing the Romanov family crest. For business reasons he did not go by his royal title, the Prince of Kiev, but called himself Graham Laing-Black. He was a good friend to us and offered to put us up in Bayswater with his aunt, the baroness, to be closer to the airport on the morning of our departure.

On entering her house the first impression was one of darkness, though when accustomed to the light one could see that it was filled to capacity with beautiful antique furniture, glass and china, which I am sure had not seen a duster for many a year! She was very charming, though as she spoke only Russian, and hardly any English, she appeared rather aloof. The house consisted of four floors, and was very dark and dingy, and altogether rather spooky. An opera singer inhabited the floor above and we could hear her practising arias repeatedly! Our room was on the first floor, very gloomy, with rather threadbare carpets and a four-poster bed. Mandy slept in a very old cot in the corner of the room. The whole thing seemed totally unreal, and rather bizarre – that I was in this house, flying to South Africa in the morning – it all seemed like a dream!

Graham gave Mandy a little Russian doll called Emilushka to take with her on the journey. It appeared Graham's family owned large pine forests on the outskirts of Johannesburg, and he promised he would look us up on his next visit to South Africa, which he actually did. He was very upset to find that by that time we were in the middle of a divorce, Mark in hospital having a back operation, and our lives in a total mess – we had even lost poor little Emilushka, whom Mandy had seen fit to deposit somewhere on the streets of Jo'burg.

CHAPTER 6

I was excited at the prospect of a new life in South Africa, and really thought it might work for us. The agency in London had booked us into a hotel in Johannesburg and also found a job for Mark, so I thought everything had been taken care of. The year was 1966, I was twenty-two and Mandy just a year old, and I looked forward to a future of fascinating discoveries.

Never having flown any great distance before, the flight was an exciting experience. Flying over the Swiss Alps at sunset was breath-taking, the snow-capped mountain peaks a salmon pink glow in the setting sun. Mandy was very good, and apart from the taking off and landing, which only seemed to cause mild curiosity, was not at all upset. She was a wonderfully good-tempered baby, full of smiles and beginning to take a real interest in what was going on around her.

We arrived in Jo'burg, stepping down from the plane into sweltering heat and onto shimmering tarmac. It was a wonderful feeling to be on African soil. Africa – a land with closely guarded secrets of witchcraft, dark magic and hidden powers – of laughter, dance and song. To be standing on this red earth was magic in itself for me. A welcoming profusion of red and yellow canna lilies greeted us in flowerbeds outside the airport as we left in our taxi to begin our new life – a brightly coloured promise of things to come perhaps?

We settled into the hotel and made friends with other British immigrants, particularly Paul and Jenny from England who were a nice couple and with whom we got on very well. The first disaster to hit us, however, was the fact that there was no job! The company that were supposed to be employing Mark apparently didn't need him. Luckily, he found something else reasonably lucrative as an air conditioning draughtsman, and we found a flat sharing with Paul and Jenny.

When Mark had been doing his chauffeuring job in London he had come across the American Mecom Racing Team, picking them up every day from their hotel and taking them around London. Strangely enough, they turned up in South Africa and were racing at Kyalami GP Circuit. Mark and I went over to Kyalami, which is about 15 miles outside Jo'burg, to meet the team and had a turn round the race track in one of their cars. Great fun, but the speed was a bit scary!

Drive-in movies were totally new to us, and we found them really good as we could take Mandy along quite easily, putting her on the back seat to sleep while watching the film in our car. You could buy your popcorn, chocolate and drinks etc. from a kiosk nearby, or be served by a waitress, having a tray that fitted to the window of the car, and settle down comfortably to watch the film, which was projected on to an enormous screen in front. I saw the film *Born Free* for the first time in South Africa, and every time I see it here (and I have seen it many times!) it brings back memories of those drive-in movies.

Johannesburg came into existence over a hundred years ago when gold was first discovered, creating an unprecedented gold-rush. What had initially been just open savannah turned rapidly into a bustling shanty town, then gradually as the mine bosses got richer, into the city we now know. Johannesburg has another name, Egoli, which means City of Gold. By 1875 almost 100,000 people lived there and the mines employed more than 75,000 workers. Black people from the reservations were forced to work in the mines, the men having to work for at least a year, during which time they were separated from their families and living in terrible inhumane conditions. To release their pent-up frustrations and general misery they were allowed to express themselves by dancing. This they did every weekend, and these beautiful, rhythmic and soul-stirring dances can still be seen at the mines today.

There are many different tribes in South Africa, speaking different languages. The bigger groups are Zulu, Xhosa and the Sotho, and there are several minority groups such as the Ndebele and Swasi. There are people of mixed race called 'coloureds', who are mainly descended from the Dutch settlers and the native population of the Cape. There are about a million Indians, whose forefathers came to South Africa to work on the sugarcane plantations, and the portion of the relatively prosperous white part of the South African population are mostly derived from Dutch, German or French immigrants. They are called Afrikaners and speak Afrikaans, which closely resembles the Dutch language. Of course there are now thousands of Scottish, Irish and English immigrants who came on the £10 immigration scheme, while prior to that the attraction of gold brought many earlier prospectors.

The city of Jo'burg held many interesting and fascinating sights for me, especially the African girls and women carrying impossibly huge loads on their heads! I walked behind one woman who was carrying an old Singer sewing machine on her head, and every time she turned a corner or stopped to talk to a friend, her head and body would turn but the sewing machine stayed in exactly the same spot, never moving an inch! Furniture, mattresses, cooking utensils, in fact anything you could think of, were all carried on the head. The local Africans I came across were usually warm and friendly, the women being mostly dressed in a mixture of Western and ethnic clothes. Nearly all the African men wore trousers and shirts, coming into the city from the townships by bus to work as office boys, houseboys, gardeners, drivers, house guards etc., but never anything that required a degree of brainpower, as the Afrikaner was renowned for believing the African did not really have one. The women worked as general servants, cooks and nannies in the houses of the whites.

After only a few weeks of sharing with Paul and Jenny they decided they wanted to be on their own and moved out, which left us to pay the full rent. I thought we were coping with this, until one evening Mark came home from work with a friend,

Claude, saying we had to move immediately, as we were going to be thrown out. This was a terrible shock, as although I had known we were in trouble financially, I had not anticipated having to move house in the space of a couple of hours. It had not occurred to me that Mark had just not bothered to pay the rent!

However, Claude had apparently found us somewhere else in another part of Jo'burg, the suburb of Judith Paarl – peeling paint, corrugated iron roofs and dirt roads. It was all happening again. I hated the dishonesty of it all – my life now seemed based on it. Moving Mandy around so much was not good for her, and I was beginning to get very angry at these constant upheavals. I felt lonely and cheated, having expected Africa to be so different. Where was the evidence of this beautiful country and all it had to offer? It was all out there, and I couldn't reach it. Apart from the climate, which was wonderful, I saw very little of the real Africa. What I was experiencing was poverty, in virtual slum-land, a district where only 'poor whites' were living.

I endured this for a few months and went along with the lies and promises that everything was going to be all right, but knew in my heart that this was not what I wanted for myself or my child, and began to think that I'd be better off on my own – at least I'd be in charge of our lives. I made up my mind to divorce Mark. During the frequent rows we were now having, Mark usually ended up saying 'I suppose you want a divorce', to which I usually kept silent. I called his bluff the next time it happened, however, and said 'Yes, that's exactly what I do want'. He was devastated.

Having had a lot of trouble with his back since we arrived, Mark went to see a specialist about it. He was informed he'd have to have a spinal fusion to correct it, the date of which was in a few weeks' time. I felt guilty at leaving him to cope with this on his own, but resolutely kept to my decision. I began divorce proceedings immediately and started making enquiries regarding residential hotels. I managed to find one in the area we had lived in originally, and they seemed happy to have Mandy. Everything was set for us to move, when, with impeccable timing as usual, another disaster struck. Mandy developed measles, and I had to make arrangements for her to go into an isolation hospital. This was a total nightmare. I took her to the hospital and left her there – a pathetic and bewildered little figure, sitting in a ward full of empty cots, totally alone. I began to wish I had never set eyes on Mark.

The next few weeks were spent desperately trying to hold down a job that I had fortunately acquired, going to the solicitors and court for my divorce, and to Mandy on hospital visits. Leaving my baby in hospital alone and ill was heart-breaking. I hardly had the courage to face her, to look into her eyes and expect her to accept the misery I was inflicting on her. I hated myself for this act of betrayal, and despised Mark for reducing our lives to this.

My divorce was through in eight weeks, that particular episode being quite terrifying. I waited all day from ten in the morning until four o'clock in the afternoon for my case to be heard. When I was eventually called, it was to appear in the witness box for exactly ten minutes, and it was all over. The case was heard in the High Court in Johannesburg, in front of masses of people, bewigged barristers and tiers of heavy carved oak benches and galleries, making one feel quite overpowered and insignificant in the eyes of the law.

I went straight from court to the hospital to visit Mark and to tell him about it. As I entered his ward I could see a nurse sitting by his bed, holding his hand! He said something, she turned round and abruptly got up and left. You can imagine I did not take too kindly to this, and with a few short words to Mark exited fairly rapidly. On my turning into the corridor I literally bumped into Graham Laing-Black. He was quite shocked when I told him of our present situation, gave me a kiss and wished me good luck, with an invitation to visit him when he was next in Jo'burg.

When Mandy was well enough, I took her back to the hotel with me. I had managed to find a crèche that would take her all day, as obviously I had to work to keep a roof over our heads. They kindly arranged to pick her up each morning and drop her off again at the end of the day, but after only a few weeks of putting her on the bus and picking her up, I could see that she was dreadfully unhappy – screaming when I left her, and each time I met her she was crying. I was frantic with worry about her. There was no money coming from Mark and I obviously had to keep working. Eventually, I decided to ask the Welfare

Organisation for help with looking after her, as I thought it would almost be better for her to have a stable environment without me than this dreadful trauma each day on leaving me. It would give me time to think and get myself straight.

They placed her in an orphanage, which absolutely broke my heart, and I will never forget her screams of 'Mummy', her outstretched arms and her tiny fingers splayed like starfish in a desperate attempt to draw me back, as they took her from me. My journey back to my one room in a hotel was one of numbness, and a leaden heart. I had taken her there in a taxi, and asked the driver to wait for me. He must have wondered what was going on, as I remember sitting in the back of the taxi desperately trying to silence the choking sobs, and with a terrible pain in my chest, as though I were going to burst. I have never felt lonelier in my life, and it all resembled a dreadful nightmare.

I began to dread my visits to her, as it took her a little while to realize who I was, with so many others constantly around her, and when she eventually did know me, it was time to leave her again. I was going to pieces without her, thinking that if I didn't do something soon I might possibly lose her altogether.

Without thought for any possible danger, I walked the streets of Jo'burg at night, looking for Mark. I began to remember the good times we had had, and the feeling of being loved and belonging. There were no strong arms around me any more and no sympathetic shoulder to cry on. The bars and clubs we had frequented became possible places to find him, but I never did, and this increased the emptiness inside. He must have been able to start a new life, and I was left behind. I became resigned to being alone, and believed that any future Mandy and I had would be entirely down to me.

While I was staying in the hotel, our South African friend from Windsor, Eric, managed to get in touch with me. How he found me I don't know, but we had a couple of dates, and then he suggested we go on a short weekend safari to the Skukuza Camp in the Kruger National Park. This was at last a chance to see a bit of Africa that was real, and too good to miss, though I wasn't quite sure how I was going to deal with the fact that I didn't really fancy him! Although I thought I knew him fairly well, I was not too sure of his intentions. However, we set off in his Mini on this promising trail of African wildlife.

We drove through the night, as the sun was too hot to travel during the day, and arrived very early in the morning at a waterhole a few miles outside the camp, in time to witness wildebeest, springbok and Thompson's gazelle enjoying their early morning drink, and close enough to hear the slurping of tongues in the cool water, and the snorts of content. We drove on, crossing a narrow wooden bridge over a river, which was teaming with hippopotamus, whose ungainly bulk looked positively graceful in the muddy water. We stopped on the bridge to watch them, and they yawned at us in lazy curiosity, or was it perhaps a warning to be on our guard? On arrival at the camp we proceeded to get ourselves settled into a *rondavel* (round thatched hut). Eric had said we'd have separate sleeping arrangements – but it didn't look very separate to me, and was the beginning of a rather disastrous weekend as far as relationships go! However, we had come to see the animals and, relationships aside, that's what I intended to do.

We were looking for lion, but unfortunately we had just missed the pride, which had been there the day before. We did manage to see them in the distance, but thought we ought not to attempt to get any nearer by leaving the dirt road, possibly to get stuck in a rut, so had to drive on. Instead we found warthogs, vervet monkeys, elephant and wildebeest. The monkeys were fascinating and quite endearing to look at, though they have vicious teeth, which can inflict quite a serious wound. They leapt all over the car chattering furiously, and one mother and baby sat on the wound-down window of the car (not really to be recommended) a few feet from me, and I was able to catch her on film.

Elephant seemed to be the most plentiful animals and we spent most of the day with them. We were on a dirt track going back to camp in the early evening, when suddenly up on the bank to the right was a large bull elephant. We stopped to watch him, but we could see that he was very disturbed by our presence. He started raising his head and trunk, flapping his ears, and bellowing his annoyance, taking a few steps back, then a few forward in mock charges. Both of us agreed that it was time for a quick exit, upon which the car stalled! I was getting quite frightened by now; in fact I was on the verge of sheer panic. I think the only thing that stopped him charging was the fact that he was on a sort of plateau, which didn't give him a clear run. We eventually got the car started and shot off in a cloud of dust!

I'm afraid by the next day Eric and I weren't speaking to each other, as I still stuck to my separate sleeping arrangements, and he obviously wasn't too happy about this. I went on a reconnoitre of the camp on my own after breakfast. I had a sneaking feeling that some of the chaps from the hotel were also there. I had heard them talking a couple of days ago that it would be a good idea. In fact, I had rather steered Eric in this direction on purpose, hoping they would be there in case of trouble! Sure enough, Mike (with whom I'd quite often had breakfast and evening meals in the hotel) was playing cricket with some others, and seemed quite happy to see me. He was a nice chap, and easy to talk to. I explained what was going on with Eric, and he offered to take me back to Jo'burg without further ado. I did feel very guilty at this turn of events, but Eric presumed too much!

Mike and I began to see quite a bit of each other, and he would take me to see Mandy when I wanted to go. He was also recently divorced, so equally lonely. He was solid and reliable, just what I needed at this time, and we didn't expect too much from each other.

Being young and not terribly interested in politics I took only a vague interest in the political situation in South Africa. I shall try to fill in the gaps a bit now (knowing much more now than I did then). Whilst working at the ESCOM Centre (Electricity Supply Commission) in Jo'burg I witnessed an extraordinary drama unfold, when minding my own business and getting on with my work as a secretary and typist, a figure came flying through the double doors to the office screaming 'He's dead, he's dead, the Prime Minister's dead. He's been stabbed. He's dead!' Of course everyone stopped what they were doing and looked around at each other in shocked disbelief. The Prime Minister, Hendrek Frensch Verwoerd, had been Prime Minister from 1958 until this moment in September 1966, and had indeed been stabbed!

Apparently, he had entered the House of Assembly that day just after lunch and, as he made his way to the front bench, he exchanged greetings with those around him, and then on taking his seat a uniformed parliamentary messenger, Dimitri Tsafendas, walked briskly across the floor from the lobby entrance. Without warning Tsafendas drew a sheath knife from under his clothing, bent over Verwoerd and raised his right hand high into the air. With his left hand, he plucked off the sheath and then stabbed Verwoerd four times in the chest. Verwoerd was given the 'kiss of life' to no avail. He was dead on arrival at hospital. Never having come across anyone being assassinated before, this came as rather a bloodcurdling shock, and it began to sink in that I was living in a dreadfully disturbed country, and that the possibility of one's life being taken was all too evident, if in the wrong place at the wrong time. Black Africans do not have the same reverence for life that we do, seeing death all too frequently in their own lives, through drought, disease, tribal wars, famine (and now AIDS). Death was readily accepted as almost a daily part of life. Not surprisingly the black Africans had reached such a fevered pitch of hate for this man and his tyrannical policies concerning them, that only his death could rid them of their suffering.

Verwoerd was not born in South Africa but emigrated with his parents from The Netherlands. He is considered to be the primary instigator of apartheid, and was Prime Minister during the Sharpeville Massacre and the banning of the African National Congress. Numerous major roads in towns and cities in South Africa that were named after him have now been changed to something more appropriate. Verwoerd is called the architect of apartheid for his role in shaping the implementation of apartheid policy when he was Minister of Native Affairs during the early 1950s, describing it as a 'policy of good neighbourliness'.

As a member of the British Privy Council, Verwoerd understood that new changes were being undertaken in the British Empire, among the most important of which was the abandonment of Imperial policy supporting white rule in Africa. Consequently, with the foreknowledge of British Prime Minister Macmillan's upcoming 'Winds of Change' speech, Voerwoerd prepared for independence, his plan being to orchestrate a republic within the British Commonwealth. Harold Macmillan then visited South Africa, making his famous speech and criticizing apartheid, only further inflaming moves for independence among the members.

This was actually the second attempt on Verwoerd's life as in 1960 while making a speech, an anti-apartheid activist and supporter of remaining in the Empire, walked up to him and fired two shots into his face. The Prime Minister was rushed to hospital still alive. At first it was thought that he would lose his hearing and sense of balance, but these fears were to prove groundless, and he returned to public life less than two months after the shooting. His successor was Balthazar Johannes Vorster.

Christmas was just around the corner, and I dreaded it. To be alone in a hotel room without my child, no family and no friends was a grim and miserable prospect. I imagined they would all be going to their various homes including Mike, and the hotel would be relatively empty. It turned out that they were all planning to go to Margate, a seaside resort on the east coast of Africa, to spend Christmas. To my great relief, Mike asked me to go with them, and to bring Mandy with me. We would all be staying with a friend of his.

Our journey to Margate was not without mishap. We ran out of petrol in the middle of nowhere, and Mike had to walk miles back down the road with a petrol can, leaving Mandy and me alone in the car. I was quietly sitting there talking to Mandy, when something caught my eye in the driving mirror. It was an African in full leopard-skin tribal dress, and he was fast approaching the car. I began to get extremely nervous – there was no traffic on the road, no-one in sight, and I had no idea where we were. I wound up the windows and sat and waited for him to pass. Of course he didn't! He tapped on the window and pointed to the dashboard. I couldn't understand what he was saying at all, until he made smoking actions with his hands indicating the cigarettes on the dashboard! I gingerly wound down the window a little, and gave him a cigarette – he gave me a broad grin and wandered off into the blue!

I'm afraid it wasn't too long before Mike made the decision to go back to his wife, and I was on my own again. I missed him – he had been good for me, and I had possibly been good for him at the time.

After about a couple of months, one of the girls at work informed me that she was vacating her place in a house sharing with six Australian girls, and I could have it if I wanted it, though she warned me that it was rather a 'bitchy' environment. I thought I could cope with this, and went to see the girls. They all agreed that Mandy would be no problem as long as she didn't interfere with their parties! It was a lovely bungalow, with a swimming pool and tennis courts, also servants' quarters, which meant that I could get a live-in nanny for Mandy. I bought a cot and got everything ready for her. I picked her up from the home and we began life again together. I thought at last things were going to work out for us.

Life in the house was quite an experience – endless parties and barbecues and company all the time, which was good for me, though there were always fights when people had taken the wrong food from the fridge or hadn't paid the rent on time. We had an ex-Olympic swimmer and a failed ballet dancer who pirouetted around the house crying 'Willow, willow', with her lesbian partner, also a professional swimmer, looking on rather bored. There was a very neurotic female, who was usually the cause of the arguments, and two other reasonably normal Australian sisters. We had just one chap living in a caravan at the back, who must have been in his element I should think. Being the only male, he fell prey to frequent nightly visits from various individuals in the household. In fact, it's a wonder he got any sleep at all!

I managed to get a nanny for Mandy, and things settled down fairly nicely. I was happy that she could be at home all day. She had the run of the garden, under the supervision of the nanny, who had strict instructions never to let her near the pool.

Everything went quite well, except that one never knew who would be staying in the house from one moment to the next, or who one might be having breakfast with! The constant noise and confusion did not seem to bother Mandy, but it obviously was not an ideal place for a child. We did a few things together as a group such as going riding, which was rather a daunting experience as the horse I was given was an absolutely huge chestnut gelding, virtually beyond my control.

I seemed to be put in the charge of some German chap, I can't really remember why, but he was an extremely abrupt military sort of fellow who all but completely ignored me, obviously thinking I was a bungling idiot! Another of our outings was to the 'mine dances' held at the Western Deep Level Gold Mine just outside Jo'burg. These dances were quite spine-tingling to watch, giving one goose-bumps to think they had been practised for so many years. This particular mine is one of the deepest in the world, going down to approximately 3,900m. Mining at this depth brings considerable problems, namely the intense heat and also humidity.

On arriving home from work one day, I discovered a woman on the doorstep waiting for me. She was from the Welfare Organisation. Apparently Mandy had been found wandering outside the front gate. A busy main road ran past the house, and she could easily have come to dreadful harm. The nanny had been drunk, and had fallen asleep, and one of the girls had reported it. I was horrified, not only that the nanny had been drunk in charge of my child, but also that the girls had seen fit to report it instead of coming to me first. They knew how much I loved her and the possible consequences of their actions.

I couldn't find another nanny at such short notice, and I lost Mandy again, back into another children's home. I really was desperate by now, unable to see any way out of this nightmare, and I could certainly not afford the fare home to England.

Through one of the parties in the house I met a lovely man, Peter, who was separated from his wife, and seemingly attracted to me. As he was still haggling over property etc. with his wife, and his mother did not approve of me (I think she wanted to see her son's marriage patched up and considered me an interference), this unfortunately came to nothing. I am sure, however, that if I had not still been in love with Mark, things could have gone a lot further. He had everything to offer, coming from a well-established white South African family, owning his own farm and comfortably off. Sometimes in the evenings we would take the Land Rover into the bush, with Mandy on my knee, and head for the nearest waterhole to watch the animals come down for their evening drink, and to enjoy the breath-taking sunsets. Africa is at its most beautiful at sunrise and in the evenings, when it seems to feel raw and untouched, and the full power of its magical beauty absolutely fills your soul. This all sounds rather intense, but I shall never forget the way Africa made me feel.

I was actually beginning to succumb to the idea that I might have a possible chance of happiness in this country, when Mark appeared on the scene to dispel any such thoughts! He turned up late one evening at the house, out of the blue. Apparently he had been offered a job in Port Elizabeth, and begged me to consider trying again. I refused, and he then proceeded to try to make me jealous by having a relationship with one of the girls, until he realized that I wasn't affected by this display of misplaced affection! He approached me again about getting together. I thought it over very carefully, and decided that, for Mandy's sake, I had to go back, but on condition that we had a trial run for six months, and if he put a foot wrong we would call it off. He assured me things would be different this time, and that he had changed, and desperately wanted us both back in his life. Looking at our present life and its surroundings, I came to the conclusion that our being together as a family was of more importance. Mandy needed us both.

Mandy and I stayed with Peter (and his mother) the night before leaving, in a *rondavel* annexe next to the main house. Dinner that evening was very formal, consequently making me rather nervous. The large oval dining table, covered in a white damask tablecloth, was laden with what appeared to be the entire collection of family silver – soup tureen, water jug, entrée dishes, beautiful sparkling lead crystal glasses and carafe, and in the centre a wonderful lavish floral display of white roses and lilies arranged in a crystal bowl. All terribly elegant and quintessentially English! The servants attending were all resplendent in white tunics and trousers with cummerbunds and fezzes of deep red. Hardly any conversation accompanied the meal, and in the end it became so embarrassing that I found myself praying for it soon to be over! Rather than being in the middle of Africa, we might well have been dining splendidly in a country house in England.

Mark went on ahead to find accommodation, and get things organized. In the meantime, Peter implored me not to go, and kept repeating that he loved me. He saw me on to the train the next day for Port Elizabeth, and on its departure from the station walked along beside it, and through the window told me he loved me, and that I was 'doing the wrong thing'!

I started my journey in tears, torn between security and happiness with Peter and my love for Mark, knowing that life with him was going to be fraught with anxiety and insecurity. I held on tightly to Mandy, and desperately hoped God was on my side.

126 Oxford Road, Johannesburg S.A.

Charging elephant in Skukuza Camp,
Kruger National Park, S.A

Jane with Amanda, Port Elizabeth S.A.

'Sheet' party - Oxford Road, Johannesburg.

Mine dances, Western Deep Level Gold mine. Johannesburg 1967.

Western Deep Level gold mine Johannesburg 1967.

Tread softly as you tiptoe through the chambers of my mind
And wander down the corridors of time
A heart cannot be broken lest the shaft be of a kind
To pierce the very soul of what is fine
Be wary with your flattery and curb your eagerness
Be gentle when these passions you explore
Have patience in abundance and treat with tenderness
A being that is fragile to the core
In your hand this heart of innocence you hold
Betrayal not an option in the scheme
A coffer full of treasure, with a secret yet untold
Tread softly – lest you trample on my dream

CHAPTER 7

Mark had not been able to find a flat in Port Elizabeth in time, and had booked us into the King's Head Hotel, which was situated at the top of a hill behind the town, with a wonderful view of the bay. We stayed here for about three weeks in all, until we eventually found quite a nice flat just around the corner. It was in an old building but unfortunately with no garden, just a back yard where the servants' quarters were. It had burglar proofing on the windows, which a number of the houses had to keep out intruders, and although it was designed to keep people out, it always made me feel like a prisoner in my own home, and was very claustrophobic.

Mark's job as an air-conditioning draughtsman was going well, and we'd managed to find a lovely African nanny called Jane for Mandy, who was quite convinced Jesus had sent us to her! She was wonderful with Mandy, strapping her onto her back with a large towel while doing the daily chores. Mandy usually fell asleep to the gentle swaying of Jane's body, and they formed a close bond. When the housework was done, Jane used to sit her down beside her on the back doorstep and they made bead necklaces together, which I held on to for a while for safe-keeping but have now given to Mandy.

On the odd occasion Jane brought her daughter Miriam to help when she had a day off school or on school holidays. Miriam, a pretty girl of about fifteen, had an air of strong resentment about her. Unlike her mother, she showed no respect for anyone, particularly a white person, and it was all too evident that her hatred for the white man in Africa burned in her soul, clouding her entire life. She had ambitions of her own, which, although she knew were far from possible to achieve, did not include a servile role such as her mother's! She would stand by the sink, her hands deep in soapy water, a sullen expression on her face, and any attempt on my part to lighten the atmosphere or to encourage a smile fell on deaf ears, until I gave up and let her get on with it. This aura of resentment seemed to permeate the entire flat until I felt quite embarrassed and guilty at being there at all! It was a shame as my attitude, not having been brought up in a black/white environment, was one of friendliness and interest, and I was not the enemy she thought me to be. Though to her, and thousands of young black Africans like her, I had a white skin which was enough – not that they didn't have a reason to hate!

Jane, on the other hand, was warm and friendly. She became close to all of us, and having a lovely sense of humour she and I would laugh at funny things that had happened either to her or to me. In the kitchen one day she tried to teach me Xhosa (the native 'click' language). By the end of my first lesson, we were both in complete hysterics, shaking with silent laughter, at my attempts to get the click right!

Resigned to her lot in the scheme of things, she was happy in her work, never complained, and apologised for her daughter's rudeness. However, the antagonism was not always a black versus white problem.

At weekends fights would break out in the servants' quarters after considerable quantities of 'Kaffir' beer had been consumed (a milky, watery alcoholic liquid made from maize – the term 'Kaffir' being a derogatory and insulting name given to black Africans by the whites and meaning 'infidel'). Violent knife and axe attacks were not uncommon. Tempers and frustrations ran high in Africans whose role in life seemed only to be one of servitude, and the loss of their land and culture were all too apparent.

Nelson Mandela, their saviour, had been imprisoned on Robben Island, and their hopes and dreams shattered temporarily, but their resolve strengthened. South Africa was in turmoil, and the unrest and racial hatred was all consuming in the townships around Johannesburg; the desperate cries of '*Uhuru*' (freedom) resounding round these shanty towns – Soweto, Alexandria and others. The crowding, squalor and poverty in these ghettos during apartheid had to be seen to be believed. Violence and crime were the result, beyond anything the police could handle. The unrest was equally apparent in the townships surrounding Port Elizabeth.

We, as immigrants, were not aware of the extent of it, thinking only, on our arrival, that we had come to the most magical country on earth, eager to explore its mystery, culture and breathtakingly raw beauty. We did not understand the complexities of a demoralized and oppressed people struggling for identity, and had viewed it until then with a detached concern, never realizing the full extent of their pain. The pride and strength of their race had been dimmed, but the war cries echoing round the hills made by Shaka Zulu and his warriors, who had led them into battle in the distant past with shield and *assegai*, still rang in their hearts, as did the memory of a parched earth vibrating to the rhythmic pounding of a thousand feet.

I had always imagined Shaka Zulu to have been a noble warrior and one to whom allegiance was willingly given, but no, far from it. Towards the end of the eighteenth century, and all over southern Africa small tribal groups were amalgamating into larger communities. This was obviously not a peaceful process, and Shaka rose to fame in this period of the rise of the Zulu Kingdom. Through incredible atrocities and cruelties Shaka gained control over several Zulu clans, raiding villages and burning them down. Women and children were killed and the young men were forced into allegiance, the chiefs tortured into surrender.

Shaka was the illegitimate son of the Zulu chief Senzangakhona and a young girl called Nandi. Under his rule the Zulu territory greatly expanded, and at the beginning of the nineteenth century Shaka had created the most powerful kingdom in the whole of southern Africa. The cruelties against his enemies became increasingly outrageous, until eventually he was assassinated by his half-brother Dingane in 1828. As a result of his reign thousands of people had become refugees and fights between the new settlers in the country and the refugees broke out everywhere. At the time of white settlement of the Cape, Xhosa groups were living far inland. From around 1770 they encountered Trek Boers who approached from the west. Both the Boers and the Xhosa were stock-farmers, and the competition for land resulted in many quarrels and ultimately wars. The more the white colony developed into a government- run state the more they tended towards a policy of white control and of land annexing, with strong suppression of the black community.

A modern 'democratic' state was formed in which only the white population retained the right to vote. The black people were subjected to a policy of concealed expatriation, and were allocated parcels of land. No white person was allowed to purchase land there and vice versa; no black was allowed to buy land in the white-designated area. So apartheid was laid down. The policy of total racial separation was introduced limiting black workers exclusively to menial work, therefore guaranteeing cheap labour. Marriage or any love relationship between the races became forbidden; everywhere segregation was introduced – all public institutions and offices, public transport and public lavatories having signs of 'Blankes' and 'Nie Blankes', whites and non-whites, displayed above their doors and on park benches. Black children's education was also repressed in case they got 'above themselves'.

Deprived of the right to vote or to strike, the ANC, the

African National Congress, was formed and several other resistance and liberation movements grew up to retaliate against black suppression. Nelson Mandela became a prominent figure in the fight for freedom, with his struggle for his people ending in 1964 with his imprisonment on Robben Island for a term of twenty-one years (his full prison term was twenty-seven years, some of which was spent in other prisons).

This was the state of affairs when we found ourselves in this beautiful part of the world, knowing nothing of its history, having been told only of the wonderful weather and the freedom of this up-and-coming society and the prospect of success being guaranteed in any job we chose. It was a young people's country, they said, and emigration to this Promised Land was greatly encouraged.

These noble people were impotent in the face of politics and the colour of their skin, but things were changing, with the old ways of battle adapting to a modern age. Instead of proud warriors menacingly beating their shields and stamping their feet to long remembered battle cries, the arena was of concrete and steel and far more impenetrable, but nevertheless politicians of the outside world were exerting pressure on South Africa to change its policies on apartheid. They were having to listen, as the riots grew to uncontrollable proportions and would not be stilled. This time black Africans would not back down, no matter how many were imprisoned or killed, or how many atrocities were performed on both black and white people, regardless.

Despite this undercurrent of unrest, ordinary people

tried to go about their normal daily lives as far as possible, with only the odd incident being reported in the paper or coming to our attention by some other means. We did have an elderly friend whose car was stoned by black Africans on the roadside as she was driving home one day, which, although she was unhurt, shook her up considerably.

Nelson Mandela is now free, having been released on 11 February 1990, and continues to be an iconic ambassador for peace, harmony, unity and freedom. A truly gifted and lovely man, and one who has done so much for his people and their acceptance into our modern world, and he will be hard to replace. He is like a god among his people and they love him – in fact he is loved and revered all over the world. He became President of South Africa in 1994, having won the Nobel Peace Prize in 1993. Mandela has often credited Mahatma Gandhi for being a major source of inspiration in his life, for his philosophy of non-violence and the dignity with which he faced his opponents.

Before too long I was able to get a job with an insurance company, and our lives were really going quite well. Mark brought home a lovely Irishman one day whom he'd met in a bar, and who proceeded to introduce fun and laughter into our lives. Paddy was a big burly man, with hawk-like good looks, and I was immediately drawn to him and his ebullient nature. One could not have him in the house without knowing it. He was generous and caring, but mad as a hatter, especially after a few drinks, which was quite often! He owned a cabin cruiser, the *Maybe*, which was moored in the harbour. Mark and I went on a few fishing trips with Paddy on board her, but caught nothing of any significance. There was a deep-sea fishing chair bolted to the aft deck for fighting marlin, shark etc., which Mark strapped himself into expectantly, but obviously to no avail.

Sharks bred in the harbour at Port Elizabeth, and you could see them quite clearly swimming around. I actually ate shark steak once, Mark having caught it in the harbour – never again, quite horrible! Although I am a good sailor, I am happier on dry land. The open ocean with no land within sight does not thrill me; in fact it gives a feeling of extreme vulnerability and dread! I feel it's rather like being lost in a desert of barren dunes stretching to infinity. I must have been a grave disappointment to my sea-loving father.

Paddy really was a light in our lives, but having said that, I am reasonably sure that he was involved in all kinds of rather dodgy dealings, with a strong element of danger attached. When Mark was away on business in Windhoek one time he brought us round a take-away for dinner, and after doing the washing up and putting Mandy to bed, he pulled me to one side and said 'Give me your hand'! I complied, and he turned it palm upwards, slowly unclenching his other hand to pour about a dozen small, sand-coloured stones into my cupped one. 'ROUGH DIAMONDS' was all he said. I was holding in my hand a veritable fortune, which was quite awesome; I also imagined they had not come by any legal route, therefore I asked no questions!

It is fascinating and perhaps quite disturbing to think that those inconsequential little pieces of sandy crystal would soon be polished up to twinkle and sparkle around some glamorous woman's throat or adorn an elegant finger, having cost many thousands of pounds, as perhaps they had sadly even cost the lives of those who mined them, and in this case possibly smuggled them, before nestling here in my palm. It was with great reluctance that I gave them back!

The following day he took Mandy and me to the Addo National Park, a game reserve. It was a wonderful feeling of utter freedom, bumping around in a Land Rover over humps in the dirt roads with the dust flying up in red clouds behind us as we drove. A breath-taking panorama of beauty spread itself around us, with the African sun beating down transforming our skin to a glowing coppery brown, kudu and springbok just lifting their heads in curiosity as we passed. The Addo Park is mainly taken over by elephant on a conservation programme, and after driving around for a while looking mostly at elephant and the odd giraffe, we returned to the station to watch the elephants having their tea. Apparently they loved oranges, and tons of these were thrown down a shoot, and the elephants caught them at the bottom. We watched from the safety of a raised wooden platform high above them.

Paddy often took me out in the evenings when Mark was away, for the odd drink at a hotel if I could find a babysitter, who was usually the woman in the flat above us. Mark didn't seem to mind, in fact encouraged it – perhaps not such a wise attitude to have taken! Once a year Paddy went on a hunting trip up north, and on one of these he brought me back a kudu skin and a wonderful large lump of amethyst, which he had found lying on the ground. This I had made into a ring and earrings, which, funds being as they were, I could never collect!

I accompanied Mark on one of his trips to Windhoek, staying the night with a family friend of his boss. They were really lovely people, kind and thoughtful, though we did encounter one or two odd things, such as the loo. This was a wooden shed-like construction at the bottom of the garden, basically a wooden box seat with a hole in it! On seeing this I felt that I couldn't really expect Mandy to use it in the middle of the night if she needed to go, and asked for a potty for her. However, we had to use it and this was done with some trepidation I can tell you, as there were plenty of snakes around! The so-called garden had been left to run wild and consisted of dry, waist-high scrub with a narrow dirt path running the length of it ending up at the foot of this noble shack – snake paradise! However, a quick dash there and back seemed to be the answer, and no snakes were encountered. We were given a wonderful breakfast the next morning, however, of pumpkin and bacon, a combination I hadn't tried before and found delicious.

I was rather keen on learning to drive, and Paddy took me out in his car one day, on a dirt road out in the veldt. It was during this so-called lesson that I experienced a rather strange thing. I was driving along, feeling quite pleased with my newly acquired abilities, when suddenly there loomed on the horizon a very large boulder in the middle of the track. As I approached it, I began to make a swerve to avoid it, when the boulder leapt about six feet into the air, flew over the bonnet of the car and disappeared into the scrub! It was the most enormous toad I have ever seen!

A couple of other incidents occurred while we were in this particular flat, one being a tornado in the back garden! It was an ordinary sunny day, when all of a sudden the whole house shook and the windows rattled until I thought they were surely going to break. It felt like an earthquake, and Mark and I both clung together terrified. We looked out of the window to see a swirling funnel of dust about sixty feet high, all the loose timber and cardboard from boxes etc. and everything movable being swept high into the air, swirling menacingly above our heads. We fortunately had burglar-proofing on the windows so were not too worried about them breaking as the mesh acted as a barrier. Had it not been there I think they would have blown in. It only lasted about two minutes, and then seemed to move on. It was a really terrifying experience.

On another occasion, when the rains came in Port Elizabeth, we were totally flooded out. I had never seen tropical rain before. It was like glass sheets, coming straight down out of the sky, and it rained continuously for several days. The water started pouring down the chimneys and we had to put towels in front of the grates to soak it up. We were getting a little worried about an elderly friend of ours who lived about a mile away on the sea front. Mark donned Wellington boots, and as much waterproof clothing as he could muster, topped with an umbrella, and set off to see if she was all right. However, he couldn't get very far, as half the sea wall had been washed away during the night, and an avalanche of water and mud had come down from the hills carrying cars etc. in its wake. Several people lost their lives in this disaster. Our friend Josephine (by this time approaching seventy) had been very frightened at the rapid rise in water but it had thankfully not reached her and she was unhurt.

Another thing we seemed to be plagued with was cockroaches. I would chase them round the flat with insect repellent, mostly to no avail. I think they built up a resistance to it in the end, and just continued to scuttle around with loads of powder on their backs! However, in the shed outside we stored all the empty lemonade and Coke bottles, and one day I went into the shed with the intention of clearing it out. I started moving the bags and to my horror, thousands of cockroaches started pouring out of the bottles and cascaded all around me! I was absolutely petrified. They were not the little cockroaches that you find in this country, but three or four times bigger! Needless to say, I made a dash for the house and let them get on with it!

As well as sea-fishing on the beach at Port Elizabeth, Mark was told that the fishing was excellent at Hartebeesport Dam. We packed up a picnic and headed for the dam one Sunday morning bright and early, with Mandy on the back seat of the car in charge of the picnic and rugs. In those days there were no seat belts and in fact in this case there was hardly any traffic to warrant any, the main roads being well-surfaced and virtually traffic free. On arrival I spread the rug and got out some little games to play with Mandy while we watched Mark doing his best to catch a fish. After about an hour or so something made me turn round, and to my absolute horror a herd of buffalo was standing only a few yards away from us – about thirty of them, and all staring in our direction! I yelled at Mark, hoping desperately that he could hear me against the wind that had got up, and began frantically getting the picnic things together, bundling them all up in the rug, and half carrying, half dragging poor little Mandy towards the car. Having gained the safety of the car I took a photo of them, as they were really rather majestic looking, and from this I did a painting, which I imagine now hangs on someone else's wall somewhere in S.A.

Mark and I had been together for about six months, when he took me on his knee and said it was about time I had another baby! Although I thought it was a lovely idea, and very tempting, I wanted a ring on my finger again first. We were married in the local Methodist church in Port Elizabeth, with Paddy as best man. It was December, the middle of summer, and a happy day with plenty of sunshine and beautiful flowers around. The church was filled with the wonderful heady perfume of white chincherinchees interspersed with majestic spikey proteas (the national flower), while outside the bluebell coloured jacaranda trees were in full glorious bloom.

Cover me in sunshine
A golden cloak to wear
A fairy dell, a wishing well
And flowers in my hair
Cover me in moonbeams
A canopy of love
And in my hand a wedding band
That lights the sky above
Cover me in raindrops
To wash my cares away
A soothing shower on eager flower
I wish that I could stay!
Cover me in stardust
A galaxy to roam
A journey bright, on starlit night
And then, please – take me home

Everything to date had gone without a hitch and I was looking forward to a fresh start. My becoming pregnant quite quickly with my second baby was a lovely surprise, the birth of which everyone eagerly awaited.

I worked at my job as a receptionist for seven months before the baby was born. It was too hot for me to go on any longer as the climb from the town up to our flat was exhausting in temperatures of 90 degrees or more, and I would arrive home in a state of collapse each time. I had a threatened miscarriage at about five months, and was put to bed with bricks under the end of it and administered to by Paddy, as Mark was usually at work, and generally treated like a queen. I had a fancy for strawberries and Chinese food, with the odd pickled gherkin thrown in! I must say, I quite enjoyed my stay in bed with such undivided attention. My baby was fine, however, and everything looked as though it was going to be all right.

Our nanny Jane was thrilled at the prospect of another baby, and fussed over me greatly, though she was beginning to look quite ill I thought. She had gone a rather sallow colour, and I'm sure had kidney trouble or something similar. Just before I went into hospital to have my baby, Jane very sadly informed me that she was too ill to continue working, which came as no surprise. We were devastated at the thought of her not being around any more, as she was part of our family and we were all very fond of her. Both Jane and I cried when she left, and Mandy who adored her, felt totally bereft, not understanding at only three years old where she could have gone. It was such a shame that this had to happen, and especially when a new baby was about to arrive. Jane herself had looked forward to it so much. Also, it meant we had to find another nanny quickly, as the baby was due in a few weeks' time – just before Christmas.

Carrie came into the world to sunshine and singing crickets, which I could hear outside the window during the event, on Friday 13 December 1968. Jane managed to find a girl, but at such short notice, not a very reliable one, and when I came home from hospital, having had Carrie, she promptly walked out, refusing to wash nappies and see to another child.

Carrie did nothing but cry the first weeks of life, and my life was fraught with coping on my own with the two children, trying to keep the baby quiet enough for Mark to get enough sleep to go to work each day, and also trying to keep an eye on our financial state. Without my salary coming in, our lives were now fraught with money worries. It was a very difficult task because, as Mark lied so readily, I never knew really what was going on.

He came home with a camera one day, saying he'd found it on a park bench. When I went across the road to pay my account at the chemist (which I kept for emergencies for the baby), instead of its being the normal R8 to R10 it was R70 (R meaning Rand)! According to the chemist, my husband had bought a camera the week before.

Our flat was now starting to feel too small, and we moved into a maisonette on the outskirts of Port Elizabeth. Carrie was about two-and-a-half months old when Mark told me of a business offer he had been made by an important member of the aristocracy. This apparently involved Mark flying to the UK to look for suitable charter areas on the south coast, and to buy a yacht for that purpose. Although I was considerably taken aback at the thought of being left on my own in Africa so soon after having my baby, I agreed to his going, but only if he were able to obtain the air fare home for myself and the children. He came home that evening waving a cheque for R500 (about £250) made out to me by a woman. He left that evening after a row – I had tried to find out where he was going, what he was doing and who this woman was, and his story was not convincing.

The next morning, I left the children with my neighbour and went into the town to cash the cheque. They kept me waiting for a very long time, always a bad sign, and then informed me that the cheque had been stopped! It wasn't until I got home that it all finally hit me. I had no money, no phone, no car and no real friends to turn to – I was alone; I wasn't even sure where Mark had gone. I began to shake from head to foot uncontrollably. I tried to pull myself together and to calm down. If I could just clear my brain enough to enable me to think, there surely must be an answer. Paddy of course. We hadn't seen him for some time, but I was sure he would come. I rang him from my neighbour's phone and told him what had happened. He was appalled, and came over straight away. He took over immediately, bottle-feeding the baby and changing her, making sure we had enough to eat and generally getting me back to sanity. I don't know what I would have done if he hadn't been there.

I knew that he was very fond of me, and God knows, if I ever needed to be loved, it was then. He wanted to look after me, and tried to persuade me to stay, saying that he would find a place for us to live etc. – but I couldn't do it. I couldn't put my trust in another man, possibly to be let down again, and so far from home. It would have been a very different life from the one I'm leading now, but I couldn't take the risk, and I also didn't love him. I longed to see my parents and my home again, and the lush green of England.

With Paddy's arrival came disturbing revelations regarding Mark's trip. Apparently the source of all this money etc. was not from the above- mentioned rather distinguished person, but actually from his wife, who was paying Mark for his company! Whether the yacht charter story was true or not I do not know to this day, but on questioning Mark later, he displayed abject remorse as usual, saying he had done it for me!

Paddy bought our flight tickets and saw us off at the airport, with tears in his eyes. I knew I'd never see him again. I left everything behind, the furniture, the family silver – nothing of great value, but nonetheless passed down from generation to generation and precious to me – and all the things I had desperately tried to keep together through the upheavals of marriage and separation. All were left behind. I boarded the plane with one suitcase between the three of us, being the standard 'survival kit'.

We had a good flight back, and flying over England's familiar patchwork of green and corn-coloured fields brought a warm glow to my heart. It was lovely to be home.

We were met at the airport by Mark and his parents. What story he had told them I cannot imagine, but I had no option but to fall in with it. We went back to stay with them in Windsor while we looked for somewhere to live. Mark had begged me not to leave him over this latest deception and said he had one more trip back to S.A. to see this woman and he would then end it. I suppose, to keep me quiet, he bought me a gold cigarette lighter and a beautiful amethyst ring – which most definitely came out of her money!

I think I was in a daze over recently having had my baby and all the events that followed. I must have been out of my mind to set up with him again – but I did. He got a job with a yacht chandlery in London and we found quite a nice house to rent in Eton, just outside Windsor. Life jogged on fairly reasonably, as far as our standards went, with me continually trying to keep our heads above water. To find tradesmen knocking at the door demanding money was a common occurrence. I had now become quite adept at dealing with them and making sure that the children didn't go without. Life was uneventful for several months, with Mandy safely settled in a nursery school just down the road in the village, and we had Carrie christened, which was a family do.

I was beginning to settle down myself by now, as nothing really major happened to upset things, until one day my brother-in-law wrote and asked Mark if he would take a boat through the canals to France for him. He and my sister were living in Sardinia by this time.

Arrangements were made and Mark set off. It was planned that I would meet him in Sardinia with the children, to give us all a bit of a holiday and a change of scenery. We agreed that he would pay money into the bank for me each week. This money did actually appear two weeks running, and then nothing. No word from Mark and absolutely no money! I couldn't stay in Sardinia with Jan much longer without paying my way, not to mention the fact that my brother-in-law, who was suffering from a heart condition, was getting frantic at the possible loss of his boat. Mark eventually got in touch. The boat was safe, but they had broken down and he needed money for a new gear box. In the end it was delivered safely and Mark returned to Nice, having found another job chartering. He said that when he'd found us somewhere to live he'd send for us. Again, no word and no money, until after a couple of weeks I flew to Nice with the children to find out what he was up to. I found him in a terribly agitated and worried state, as obviously the job was not going according to plan, and after the usual row over finances, I decided that it would be better to return to England with the children, where we would be safe. Mark went and bought the train tickets and told us he had booked a couchette, also that he had wired his parents to meet us at Victoria station.

After saying goodbye and boarding the train, I discovered that we had no couchettes booked at all, and that there was no food available on the train! It was packed, and I had to struggle to find a seat for us all. Mandy was then four and Carrie only eighteen months, and I was very worried as to what I was going to give them to eat. I went along the corridor to talk to the guard, who very kindly offered his compartment and some milk and sandwiches. The journey seemed endless. We were told by the guard to stay on our part of the train in Paris and not to change, which we did. About half an hour later when the ticket inspector came round, to my amazement and panic, I discovered we were on our way to Belgium, and that I should have changed as I had thought! I had to pay extra fare, which reduced my funds to nil.

The children and I were ravenously hungry by now and

they were miserable. We all got out at the next stop and waited over an hour for the next train back to Paris, and the connection for our cross-channel ferry. It was bitterly cold and windy on the empty platform, and all of us were chilled to the bone by the time the train arrived. A very homely looking Portuguese couple sat opposite us on the train eating their lunch, and I could see the children could not take their eyes off this feast, until the woman offered them some French bread and salami! Poor little Carrie couldn't eat it at all and Mandy was not overly impressed. But I think the act of nibbling something made them feel a bit better.

We arrived at Victoria eventually, and sat on a bench to wait for Mark's father to pick us up. Nobody came. I was beginning to get very worried as I had no money with which to get us home – just enough for a phone call in fact. I rang his parents to find out what had happened. They had absolutely no idea we were in the country, let alone sitting waiting to be picked up at Victoria station! When I came out of the phone booth after making the call, we went back to the bench to sit down again and wait. I suddenly realized I had left my bag in the phone booth in my panic and confusion. It had everything in it – my passport, keys, South African identity card, and everything that I normally carried around with me. It was nearly six o'clock, and the lost property department was just about to close, but thankfully I just got there in the nick of time. Someone had only just handed it in thank goodness, and what honesty! By the time Mark's father eventually arrived, the children were both crying, we were all horribly dirty from travelling, and all of us starving. He took us back to Windsor, where we waited for Mark.

Weeks and then months went by, with only the occasional phone call from Mark with some feeble and implausible story. The latest yacht he was skippering had broken down, they'd run out of fuel, the weather was bad etc., and he couldn't get home. I stayed in Windsor with his parents, got myself a job and a crèche for the children, until I decided to return to Devon and my parents. They had retired there whilst we had been in S.A. and had a small cottage on Appledore quay overlooking the River Torridge. I proceeded to divorce Mark for the second time.

Though cramped in the cottage, it was lovely to see my parents again and to feel totally safe. I hadn't seen them since Carrie's christening, which seemed a very long time ago. It was a good and healthy life for the children, being near boats and the sea, with their grandparents as added security. Both Mandy and Carrie now tell me that they looked on this as their home. I suppose this is the only secure place they can ever remember.

My father had built a cabin cruiser by that time, and the children loved going up and down the river, playing 'house' below deck and handing up pretend cups of tea for the 'captain'. My father was very good with them, and the little things he would do with them reminded me of my own childhood. Only I think he had more time for them than he had had for me! He took them crabbing along the quay, with a bucket and a piece of string with a bit of bacon on the end of it, and we did Sunday trips out into the country picking blackberries. In the summer we often went to the Turners' farm, where he had frequently been as a boy, being great friends with John Turner, the nephew of the two aunts who ran the farm. He would escape his aunt and cycle out there to get away from home.

John had married Mary, a lovely woman and a great friend to my mother. We loved the teas they gave us, with mountains of clotted cream and the biggest sponge cakes I ever saw. My father would take the children round the farm inspecting the sheep and cows and a curly-headed bull they kept chained up in a barn. This brought back memories of my own childhood, being hoisted onto the enormous Shire horse that did the ploughing, my legs splayed at right-angles over his huge bristly back. The children loved Appledore, especially in the summer when they could go to the beach and poke contentedly around in the rock pools. Unfortunately, this was to be a fairly short-lived heaven.

I obtained a job in the local shipyard in Appledore without too much trouble, and the next four years were spent in, thankfully, normal existence and peace of mind, as far as I was concerned.

CHAPTER 8

One summer Jan and her children came to stay for a while, in a bed and breakfast round the corner from the cottage. On going out together one evening, we met David. We were sitting at a table in a bar having a drink, when Jan mentioned there was a man at the bar who had been looking at me for the last half hour! We introduced ourselves and it transpired that he was a maths teacher, and had just arrived from Norfolk. He seemed rather serious I thought, but definitely nice. From then on we became an 'item'. He got to know the children, and although he was slightly stern at times, they got on well. After a fairly short time, he asked me to marry him, which I had vaguely anticipated. I accepted for many reasons – sadly the wrong ones. I thought at least here was someone I could rely on, with a good solid profession and a sense of responsibility. I knew I couldn't stay with my parents much longer, with all three of us in one room, and my parents were getting too old to have young children around them all the time. As David was a live-in housemaster, a flat went with the job.

I was on mild tranquillizers by this time, the signs of previous traumas beginning to show, and having had to go through another divorce had not improved things. David issued an ultimatum. Either I gave the tranquillizers up immediately or he wouldn't marry me! He had no idea what effect this would have, and I spent a few terrified weeks not daring to cross a road on my own, as with withdrawal setting in I could not see properly where I was going or the oncoming traffic. He was not at all sympathetic, treating it almost as a joke, and I coped with this on my own – a seed of doubt setting in.

We were married in a registry office just outside Appledore, and moved into a flat in Grenville College in Devon, where I began my life as the wife of an assistant housemaster in a public school.

I began to sense that every move I made was being watched. Scores of pairs of eyes would watch me when I hung out the washing, or if I sat in the garden. There were classrooms all around me, and as a result, privacy and a life of my own seemed to be a luxury of the past. I also felt other teachers and their wives were judging me as an unsuitable candidate for such a position, being rather fashion conscious I suppose, and more a member of the outside world than this inner sanctum! Though they were all pleasant enough, I had nothing in common with any of them, except perhaps my children.

One thing I discovered very early on was that David was an extremely jealous person. A man only had to look at me for him to be very annoyed. It caused moody silences in pubs and several pointless rows at home. When I look back on my life with David, I realize I was not myself at all – just someone trying to make the best of a bad bargain, and desperately willing the world to be right. I was not the one for David, and he certainly wasn't right for me. He was an only child, had never been married before, and knew nothing about bringing up children, in fact nothing about children. This makes one wonder why he ever became a teacher at all! To marry without love had been a terrible mistake, and I was paying a high price.

He seemed set on destroying my poor little Carrie – not Mandy so much, as she was nearer in age to the boys he taught, and he could relate to her more easily. Mandy also was good at sports, joining in with the boys playing hockey at the weekends, which he supervised. He was sarcastic to Carrie, which she was too young to understand, and would twist the things she said into something that made her look silly. Everything she did seemed to be wrong in his eyes, until instead of being a happy little girl, and a bit of an extrovert, she began to change, becoming sullen and quiet around the flat. She would sit in a corner hugging a cushion and chewing the corner of it. I'm sure that because she looked so like Mark he was jealous of her and the more I sprang to her defence, the more jealous he became. He would purposely ignore her when she needed his help or attention.

Snow arrived one winter, much to the children's delight, and David took them tobogganing with tea trays on the nearest hill. About an hour after they'd left, Carrie arrived home on her own crying with misery, her face, hands and feet purple with cold and soaking wet. She developed a dreadful cough after this episode, and I would lie awake at night listening to her coughing and praying she wouldn't wake him with it. He would be very angry if this happened, and instead of sympathizing with her, would scold her for the noise she was making. He took a group of boys on a skiing trip to Austria one year, and was very worried at the thought of me being on my own – not I suspect because I might be lonely, but rather that I might go out on the town without him, or worse, have a wild affair! His first words on returning were 'Have you been faithful?'

Life was becoming claustrophobic with the constant presence of the boys, and I now had to cope with David's jealous possessiveness, which seemed to haunt him. He had no reason to feel this way, as I most definitely gave him no cause for this irrational behaviour.

I was getting very worried about the situation, and mulled over the idea of having another baby. Perhaps if he had a child of his own it would take the heat off Carrie. Though it wasn't always just Carrie who suffered. He sat them both down to lunch one day to stuffed heart, which he had prepared himself, and told them they could not leave the table until they had finished it. Both of them were retching over this ghastly meal until I put a stop to it. I swept up the plates and threw the whole lot into the bin, and told the children to go outside. For the first time in our marriage I completely lost my temper, daring him ever to treat my children like that again, or I would leave him. For once his air of superiority and arrogance left him, and I think he actually realized the misery he was causing.

It was becoming increasingly difficult for me to fit in at the school – I just wasn't one of them. As my marriage was not a happy one, I had that to contend with as well. My own school days had been generally unhappy, and I was not comfortable in that atmosphere. All the staff and wives were required to have dinner every evening in the staff dining room. This was hardly an exciting experience, as they talked of nothing but the school, the boys and exams, and I ploughed through many a meal in complete silence. In fact, I began to dread the evenings and this compulsory torture. However, in the holidays, when the boys had gone home, it was really very peaceful. The beautiful main house had belonged to the Stucley family, and my mother and I had known Betty Stucley, who had lived there as a child before it had been turned into a public school. The grounds were lovely, with carpets of daffodils in the spring and masses of flowers and shrubs in the summer. The children and I would have them to ourselves with no curious eyes to make us feel uncomfortable.

All the time I had been married to David, I had kept my job at Appledore Shipbuilders, going to and from work in the car. With the increasing worries at home, I was beginning to feel anxiety when driving. One day, on coming home, I found myself stuck in a traffic jam, panicked, and blacked out. I managed to get the car home but refused to drive again. David was very angry at this nervous collapse, and it certainly did nothing to improve the situation. He now had to drive me to work and the children to school. The more tense things became, the worse I got, and the more he took it out on Carrie.

I decided that this might be the right time to try for another baby. With this in mind, the atmosphere in the house began to change considerably, and with the prospect of a child of his own, David became more affable. I became pregnant quite soon, and it was really quite a happy time in the house, with everyone looking forward to her arrival. Even the other masters and their wives were getting excited! David looked after me very well, and was quite concerned when I insisted on working until a month before she was born. He was with me all through the initial labour, but this carried on far too long, and in the end I had to have a caesarean section. He was overjoyed when she arrived, holding her up and saying she was 'just the size of a football'. I thought everything was now going to be all right, as he was obviously thrilled with her and so were the children.

The first few months were happy ones, with the children eager to help with bathing and feeding etc., but very gradually, as David got used to the baby, his attention turned once again to Carrie. She had to wash her hands before going near Emma, and was only allowed to play with her for a short while before being told to leave her alone. Again the sarcasm began, and a sadistic teasing. I developed agoraphobia, and was terrified if anyone came to the flat or if I had to go out of it. I even had to pluck up the courage to put the milk bottles out for the milkman, because there was a classroom opposite and they could see me! In the end I was so dizzy and felt so faint, that I was afraid to hold Emma in case I dropped her. I got myself to bed and told David that I couldn't cope any more, and that he would have to ask our neighbour in the flat below to look after Emma until I could handle things again. He was silently furious, and virtually threw my breakfast tray at me the next morning, and I got the silent treatment from then on.

I staggered out of bed the next day, however, determined that my children shouldn't suffer because I was not around, and collected Emma from the downstairs flat. David now spoke to none of us, so we tried to pull together to form some sort of normality, excluding him altogether. I would not let him near me and he slept on the sofa in the sitting room.

The atmosphere was really dreadful – living in the same house and not speaking to each other was intolerable. I don't think it affected the children quite so much because they had me; but my being a fairly outgoing sort of person, also very sensitive, it affected me very much, to the point of not being able to stand it any longer. It was at this point that I went to the doctor, and found myself back on tranquillizers again.

I decided to take the children down to my sister in Cornwall, to give David a chance to come to his senses and to realize what he was doing to us all, also to give myself and the children a break. My brother-in-law had died of a heart attack in Sardinia earlier on and Jan was now living on her own with the children. My father came to the rescue as usual, and drove us all down there the next day. Jan had started up a pottery there, which was going quite well, and to be amongst my family again was reassuring. I began to feel better with no pressure on me from anyone, though I was very worried about the whole position we were in, and didn't really have an answer as to how I was going to continue. I didn't hold out much hope with regard to David changing his attitude towards Carrie, so I had no idea what I was going to do.

I was doing the ironing in Jan's kitchen and listening to the radio one day, when I happened to hear Mark being interviewed at the Boat Show in London. I began to think that it might be an idea for Carrie to go to him for a while, although he had not seen either of the children or had anything to do with us for about seven years! He had married again, and was also living in Cornwall.

I rang him and explained the position I was in, and told him what was happening with Carrie. I asked him if he and his wife Alex could have Carrie for a bit until I could sort out our future. He was very understanding about it all, and agreed that it was quite all right with him, though of course he would have to ask Alex, and he'd ring me back. I was hopeful that she would say she agreed, as this would be a temporary solution to the problem. As Mark had quite a large house in the country, with animals around, I thought Carrie would be sure to enjoy it, plus the fact that he had two more children there as company for her, being her half brother and sister.

A few hours later, he rang to say he and Alex had talked it over and had decided that it would be better for the children if they both came. I was stunned – I knew I couldn't go back to David with Carrie, and I also couldn't return to my parents, as there were too many of us by now, so in a daze I let them go to Mark. I packed a bag for them, and he picked them up the following day. I explained to them that they were going for a holiday with him and that they'd be back with me soon. I couldn't allow them to see how devastated I was. Mandy tells me now that Carrie looked up at her and said 'Who's that man?' I felt totally numb and couldn't believe it was real. I seemed to have no control over anything any more. With a heavy heart, I returned to David with just my baby, and went through the motions of day-to-day life, but I could not forgive him for the misery he had brought about, both for myself and the children.

When David had first come down from Norfolk, he had brought his cat with him. This cat had been his constant companion, and was much loved. However, it wasn't used to children, and although they had tried to win her round, she would have nothing to do with them, and took to staying out all night and wandering off for days at a time. Not too unusual for a cat in the country but David seemed to feel this very much, and thought the cat was unhappy.

One evening, when we were sitting watching television, he suddenly said to me 'I brought her into the world, and I'll see her out', at which he picked up a hammer that was lying on the table, and walked out of the room and down the stairs. Thoughts went racing through my head that he was about to do something horrific, but I tried to dismiss them by busying myself in the kitchen. Surely no-one in their right mind would actually do what I was thinking. I dismissed it as impossible.

About twenty minutes later, I could hear him coming up

the stairs. He appeared in the doorway, blood splattered all over him, the hammer hanging limply by his side, and tears pouring down his cheeks. Livid claw marks ran down his arms amongst the blood. All he said was 'She wouldn't die'. I could only gasp, 'Oh God, what have you done?' He was so distraught that I had to put my arms round him to comfort him, though I was in a state of complete disbelief and bewilderment. It took some time for the horror of it to sink in – he had actually killed his cat rather than let her 'suffer'. He waited until the evening, and then buried her in the garden somewhere.

After this episode, I thought there was something seriously wrong with him – that he was mentally unstable – and kept my distance. The thought crossed my mind that if he couldn't have me, and make me love him, I might meet a similar fate! I couldn't bear him to touch me from then on, and life was back to our not speaking to each other again. I went mechanically through a daily routine, looking after Emma and normal house duties, until one day, when I was making the bed in our room, he came up behind me, grabbed me by the shoulders, swinging me round, and threw me onto the bed. He shouted 'You're my wife', and flung my arms wide, holding my wrists in a vice-like grip. He then proceeded to rape me. I lay like a corpse, showing not one sign of emotion, though the pain in my wrists was excruciating. I had a heavy silver chain bracelet and a watch on and, with the pressure of his hands, both were gouging my flesh. I just lay there thinking – this is the end, this has finally finished it.

I waited for an opportunity when David was on house duty, and not likely to come home, packed a suitcase and rang my father to come and collect us. I was terrified all the time that David might suddenly turn up and try to stop us. I had to go across the courtyard to the main house to use the public phone, which was right underneath his room, and this proved very nerve-wracking. Luckily nothing untoward happened, and we were able to leave without hindrance. It was the end of yet another traumatic chapter in my life.

I returned to my parents yet again, with Emma, and started divorce proceedings against David. On telling them what had actually happened, my parents both just stood and looked at me. Again, there was no understanding and no arms around me. I knew that they loved me but it seemed to be impossible for them to show it with any physical demonstration of affection or tenderness. Even uttering some words of sympathy might have helped. This somehow made me feel quite 'dirty' all over again, and that the fault was mine!

David tried to win me back for a time, bringing me flowers and vegetables from the garden as a peace offering, but enough was enough, and we parted, feeling very bitter towards each other. From then on he took not the slightest interest in Emma and severed all ties, returning to Norfolk and his parents, which was a very immature and cowardly way of dealing with things. I don't think he had ever had much understanding or attention as a child. He, like Mark, was from a forces background, and this seems to create insecurity and a lack of love, a stiff upper lip being the answer to most problems. I remember once when his parents were out in Cyprus, when I hadn't really known him very long, and he was desperately worried about them, not having heard from them.

There was trouble in Cyprus at the time, and his parents were due home. He didn't know whether they were all right, and even if they had left. He was in a complete state about it, so I told him to ring his aunt, who was in England, to see if perhaps she had heard. To his amazement, his parents were there, had been for several days, and hadn't even thought of ringing him to let him know they were safe. He came back from the phone in tears.

CHAPTER 9

My life seemed to be going round in circles, getting nowhere – in fact, I was worse off each time round. I began to long to be back in Africa. I missed its untamed vastness and beauty, and the challenge and excitement of an unknown culture, the chant of the Africans digging the red earth along the roads of Johannesburg, and the vibrancy of life there – the tribal dances, and the rhythm of the drums, making one want to join in! The miners danced in an arena set aside for this purpose, from where the mostly white audience watched, their dusty brown bodies swaying and stamping to an earthy rhythm, adorned with leopard skin and feathers. War cries were offered up to the hot African sky, and shrieking whistles pierced the air. One dance they performed in Wellington boots, slapping the sides of the boots and stamping to the beat. I had yearned to be a part of Africa, and to learn so much more about its people, but had never had the time or the opportunity. I was always too wrapped up in the traumas of my own life to learn about another. If I had stayed there with Paddy, I would have had that chance, and would have had my children now. Perhaps there'll be another time for me, and I'll go back. There was no point in reminiscing, however, on what might have been – I had to move on – try to pick up the pieces and start again. Finally I could breathe again and think, although I had no idea what the future held. I desperately wanted to have Mandy and Carrie back with me, but it was totally impossible without something to offer them.

Until Emma was about eighteen months old, life ticked over. Mandy and Carrie were still with Mark, though judging from phone calls and when they came to stay with me, Carrie was not happy. Alex appeared to be a very unemotional and rather difficult person to live with, and neither of them could go to her with any worries that they had. I had unwittingly thrown Mandy into the role of mother and she felt, as she was the eldest, she had to protect her sister, and be there for her – this for a thirteen-year-old was a big responsibility, and they both must have felt very bewildered and alone. I had made things infinitely worse for both of them and worried about them constantly.

Another man entered my life at this time – Patrick. How can I begin to describe him? He came into my life like a hurricane and left behind a trail of devastation. I was out with a couple of friends one evening, and they decided that I would be the perfect match for him! They took me round to his flat in Appledore to meet him. When I first set eyes on him, I thought that his face, in repose, was very strong, but also vulnerable, and was immediately drawn to him. He was very tall, athletically built, with wild fair hair and good-looking in a Nordic sense. (It has just occurred to me that the few men I have allowed myself to care about have all had a rather 'leonine' appearance, and similar strong and sculptural features! I suppose you could say that they all, in a way, have resembled my father to a degree. Something Freudian there no doubt! However, if you think about it, boys very often are attracted to girls who look like their mothers; similarly, girls are attracted to boys who resemble their fathers. Hence I suppose the continuance of 'family resemblance' in the blood line!) He did, in fact, repeatedly remind us that he had Viking blood in his veins!

Patrick was in fact Northern Irish and quite a dramatic person really, and on entering a room, heads would turn and he made an immediate impression on people. He had an air of Irish innocence and charm about him, which I suppose brought out the maternal instinct in me. He told me about his father, who, being an avid gambler, had landed the family literally homeless, as he'd gambled away the house they lived in. His mother divorced his father and remarried. He strongly resented his stepfather, and an impossible relationship of hate developed. So much so, that it was decided that, to keep the peace, he should join the Navy. At the age of fifteen, this must have appeared to be a total rejection by his mother of her son, and this remained with him until he died. As far as I know, he had very little contact with his mother on leaving home, being unable to forgive her, and would not even go to see her in Ireland when she was dying. His father died in pathetic circumstances in poverty and squalor.

He was in the Navy until he was twenty-two, seeing action

in Korea and Borneo, attached to a special unit, and had medals for his combat achievements. He had been shot in the foot in a skirmish, and was very conscious of this disfigurement. He had a vivid imagination and a quick brain, and before I met him had started writing a book about his life in the Navy, but never finished it, which was a shame, as I'm sure it would have made interesting reading. To be a journalist or a lawyer had been possible career moves for him on leaving the Navy, but neither came to fruition. On leaving the Navy, he got involved in a very fast crowd in London, where drink and drugs were the norm, and all traces of constructive and creative thought were obliterated.

I had an understanding and an intimacy with Patrick that I didn't have with Mark or David. Although he became very jealous as time went on, and if any man in the street should happen to look at me, I received the 'third degree', and was bound, in his eyes, to have had a relationship with them. It was treated as a joke by both of us to start with, until I began to realize that he was serious in his condemnation of possible bygone affairs, and it then became irritating and annoying.

Emma was just two when I met him. He got on very well with her and vice versa. Carrie and Mandy also liked him on the occasions they came to stay, and we were very happy to start with. He was a very easy person to live with and didn't think my having three children any kind of problem. Large families are common in Ireland, and he had had younger sisters to look after as a matter of course, when they had lived in Portadown. He accepted Emma as his own, and she looked on him as her father – her own father having no contact with her at all.

As Patrick at that time had his own flat-roofing business, we had good money coming in, though at times it was erratic. We found a flat in Appledore, and to start with they were happy days. His drinking was quite heavy, but didn't seem to interfere with his work, and I suppose I accepted it as just being part of him – until one day he hit me. I can't remember what I can have said to provoke him, but it seemed to come out of the blue. It didn't stop at just being hit. I was three months pregnant with his child, and was dragged by the hair and punched and kicked until I could hardly stand. All I could do was lie on the floor and try to protect my baby. I told my parents I had fallen down the stairs to our flat, which I could see they didn't believe. This was the beginning of numerous attacks – not so much when pregnant but certainly after.

Like a fool, I married him, thinking that this incident was an isolated one, and that it couldn't possibly happen again. When he had sobered up the next morning, nothing was mentioned about it, and I came to the conclusion that he had had a blackout, and just didn't remember. I didn't dare mention it for fear of starting something else up again. We moved out of the flat into a cosy little cottage up on a hill overlooking the river, and life continued at a normal pace, until we hit a dreadful patch of bad weather. It rained continuously for weeks on end, and any roofing jobs that should have been done had to be left. Eventually, we were on the verge of starvation, and Patrick had to sign on the dole.

In the meantime, Carrie was dreadfully unhappy where she was with Mark and Alex and every time I rang her she would be in tears and begging to come back to me. I was about six months pregnant and desperately worried about our situation. Patrick was drinking really heavily by this time, but had also got a job as 'cook' on a fishing boat to occupy his time.

The phone calls from Carrie were getting desperate by now, and I knew that I had to do something to enable her to come home. I put my name down for a council house, as with a baby on the way, and another child joining us, the cottage was too small. How I could have Carrie with me with all this going on I really didn't know, but I couldn't refuse her. The council house wasn't long in coming fortunately, and we moved in within a couple of months.

There seemed to be some confusion over the due date of my baby, and I went into hospital slightly early with a false alarm. They kept me in for observation for about a week before they finally induced her. Patrick came to see me just once before I had her, bearing a box of chocolates and some flowers, and never appeared again until I returned home nearly six weeks later. I was dreadfully hurt by this, particularly at not being able to reach him while in labour. I was in labour for nine hours, which was a change from the others, and then had to have a caesarean section. Lucy was born prematurely, weighing only four pounds six ounces, very different from my other three, who had all been around seven. I named her myself, without consulting Patrick. She was very much my baby, and I didn't consider he had any right to be involved, not having been near me throughout the entire birth. These were very lonely days for me – my tiny baby was in an incubator on a drip, I was in pain, and also there was deep snow outside, which prevented anyone from coming to see me except my parents, who were wonderful. I found it impossible to explain the absence of my husband to everyone, as I could not understand it myself. To this day, I still can't think why he stayed away – unless he had been drunk all that time.

However, on my arrival home, he was so thrilled to see us that the desolation I had felt in hospital was soon forgotten. He explained his absence by saying he just had a horror of hospitals. Maybe this was true, and hospitals held some haunting reminders of some past trauma – I shall never know. This happiness didn't last long though. His drinking got worse. I tried secretly to pour the alcohol down the drain on many occasions, but he would just go out and buy more. My housekeeping money would disappear and I found it hard to cope. My life became a battle of wits with me trying desperately not to antagonize him for fear of being hit, and coping with a new baby and Emma. Carrie joined us amidst this chaos, and although it was lovely to have her, we suddenly seemed to be a family that had doubled overnight!

Patrick behaved like two people. The one I had fallen in love with was loving, generous and fun – the other one terrifying in the extreme. After a few drinks and a wrong word from one of us, usually me, he would change into an animal, with an insane look of hate in his eyes. He would become verbally abusive, sarcastic and violent, and we were all terrified of him. Every sentence in a conversation resembled a step in a minefield. One false move and the air would erupt in an explosion of vitriol and sneering accusations, transforming gentleness and love into a cunning and predatory game. Using one's wits and reflexes became the art of surviving, having to sidestep quickly, rehearse in one's head before uttering anything in case any word or sentence could be twisted or manipulated to form a threat, in which practice he took a sadistic delight. His hand would whip across the table and grab my wrist or arm in a vice-like grip, and I knew from that moment that I was going to have to defend myself.

We very seldom did anything very much together, or even as a family. We had a few outings to the beach, where we barbecued the fish he'd caught the previous day, and really that was about it as far as I can remember. His friends consisted entirely of drinking companions, whose main object in life seemed to be lifting a pint glass, and the whole drunken scene became disgusting to me. His behaviour was sadistic and violent, and any evenings out we did actually have together usually ended in a drunken argument. I gave up and stayed at home.

My days were ruled now by terror and fear. I locked Patrick out of the house on a number of occasions when he came back from the pub at night too drunk to stand. On some of these occasions he slept in the garden shed, but on another was so livid that he hurled himself at the front door and broke it down.

The neighbours came round to see if the children and I were all right, and managed eventually to calm him down. The police arrived many times when he had hit me, but could do nothing that was within the law. Now, thank God, the law has changed regarding domestic violence and battered women – some women having had the courage to speak out and be heard.

One night his friends brought him home and dumped him on the path outside. The children discovered him first thing in the morning, still lying there. Another time he passed out on the back lawn, and Carrie and I called an ambulance, hoping they would take him away, but it didn't work. Instead, he came round to find ambulance men and oxygen tanks all around him, and he realized what I had done. The police had to be called to calm him down before he took his anger out on me. He took to throwing anything he could lay his hands on at me – cans of food out of the larder etc. and once a handful of four-inch nails into Carrie's face, and if I hadn't caught his hand and stopped him, he would have hit her.

Carrie and I would act as a team – one seeing to the younger children and our escape, and the other ringing the police. We had to do this without his knowledge as, if he realized what we were doing, it would worsen the situation. Before we had a phone, one of us would have to try to get out unseen, and run to the phone box down the road to call, while the other looked after Emma and Lucy. He never touched either of them and they were spectators in this nightmare, though what effect seeing their mother continuously hit and kicked had upon them I am not sure. I think the horror has been blocked out, and both Carrie and I have developed a fighting streak in our characters that normally would not have had a chance to surface. I think if a man ever hit me again, something inside me would snap, and I would react with instinctive self-preservation. I did turn round and threaten Patrick with a kitchen knife once, but not being a naturally aggressive person I would not have followed through. I just wanted him to feel the terror that I felt, and for him to fear his life was in jeopardy. It made him stop in his tracks, and a look of uncertainty and disbelief crossed his face. I had him – just in those few seconds he was unsure.

One time he beat me up so badly that I couldn't walk. I had to go to bed and the doctor was called. Carrie had to stay off school to look after Lucy until someone from Social Services could come to help. My hands were so swollen from trying to protect my head that I couldn't hold her and I was afraid I would drop her. All Patrick said when he woke up the next morning was that I had done it to myself! He never once acknowledged or apologized for anything he did – mostly because he didn't remember – it was all a total blackout.

He was smoking cannabis as well by this time. I remember one time in a restaurant, when he had taken me out supposedly for a romantic evening, and the time came to pay the bill, whereupon instead he tipped the entire table and its contents into my lap, and just sat there laughing! I was so shocked I just got up and walked out. I left him sitting there, high as a kite, with a smile on his face, amidst the debris. When Lucy was just a baby of about three months, I was holding her in my arms whilst sitting on the bed one day, and he was shouting the usual drunken abuse at me, calling me a 'whore' and a 'tart', but then said he was going to kill me. He ran downstairs to find something heavy enough to carry this out, and came tearing up the stairs again brandishing a rolling pin. I had my back to him, and out of the corner of my eye, saw his hand go up ready to come down on my head. I decided the only option I had was to turn round and face him – which I did. He stopped mid-air. I was cold with fear. I think this unexpected confrontation of both his wife and his child saved our lives. I have thought, since these attacks, both verbal and physical, that he truly believed it was his mother he was facing, and that the pent-up anger and hurt came out in these drunken rages.

By now I had begun having a few drinks to calm myself down a bit before Patrick's impending return from the pub. I was so terrified of him by now that I couldn't think straight, and the drink helped me to relax enough to cope with looking after the children, getting their meals and trying to maintain as near to 'normal' a life as I could for them, but by this time my everyday life consisted wholly of uncertainty and fear. I began thinking of a way to kill him without being detected! I thought how easy it would be – weed-killer in a bottle of cider would go down before he realized what had hit him. He could consume virtually half a bottle with one swig. I realized that this was not the answer, however, as the children and I would be the ones to suffer in the end, and Patrick would then not only be out of the picture, but would never be aware of the harm he had done. Also, when it came to the crunch, I would never have had the cold-heartedness to carry it through.

Amidst all this drama and chaos my mother died. I missed her so much, and couldn't take in the fact that she was no longer there. She had always been there – my staunchest ally in times of need and unfailing in her love, my mentor and my guide. The future without her was bleak. I think she just gave up. Her move to Devon had been only to please my father, and I had always known that she was never happy there. When they had moved from Weston her social life became non-existent. She had left her new-found friends in the Poetry Society and the neighbours with whom she had frequent chats over tea or coffee, and the friendly banter of the shopkeepers. She had also gained some confidence in public speaking, having taken her turn in reading her own poems to an appreciative audience. All of this came to an abrupt end when they settled in a tiny village in Devon. My father very seldom, if ever, took her out of an evening, and they only seemed to go for drives in the country when the weather was sunny. She had no friends apart from Mary Turner (the wife of my father's farming friend John Turner). As my father was continually occupied in the throes of making some model, cupboard, boat, etc. she was dreadfully lonely, to the point in the end of suffering from acute agoraphobia, not being able to go only three doors down to the village shop without being accompanied. This I didn't fully understand at the time, but now realize how inwardly terrified she was actually feeling, having since felt it myself.

You could say that God moves in mysterious ways, as one night, when Patrick got up to get a glass of water, he collapsed downstairs with severe chest pains, until he could hardly breathe. He insisted he was all right, but I thought this was too serious to ignore, and called an ambulance. He was then taken to hospital, after which he had a heart by-pass operation, performed in London by Sir Magdi Yacoub.

Before he went, I told him that he would have to find somewhere else to live – I didn't want him back, and I filed for divorce. Up to now I had tried several ways of getting him to leave, but he had always turned up on the doorstep, begging for forgiveness. I had not wanted to give up my house and subject my children to a women's refuge. This house was in my name, and virtually the first one I had lived in for more than a few months at a time, while married, and I was not going to leave it.

After the operation, he rang me to say he had nowhere to live, and asked if he could come back to recuperate. He swore that he'd changed, and that his drinking days were over. I gave up in the end, as I thought he surely couldn't pose a physical threat to me any more. He was now reduced to walking very slowly and not exerting himself in any way. From a fit six-foot-three-inch strong man he was now only able to shuffle about, and his hair had turned almost white in a matter of weeks. He was a broken man, and proceeded to take it out on me. The verbal abuse and sarcasm started all over again. I told him to go, and Social Services found him somewhere to live where he could be looked after.

No more the sight
No more the sound
No more the hours of waking to the light of another day with you
No more the panic that I feel
Knowing that this life is real
And knowing it cannot be overcome unless you leave
No more the anguish for my children's sake
No more the cruel abuse I'm forced to take
No more the drunken sot within a chair
Whose brain is addled beyond care of those around
No more the anxious waiting hours when you're away
No more the terror that I feel if you should stay
No more the clearing up of broken bits
You've hurled about in violent fits of inebriated madness
No more the trembling fear inside
Knowing that we all must hide
Or be a target for your flagrant incapacity
For now you've gone, and I am free to breathe again.

CHAPTER 10

Once again a man had gone out of my life, and even with his departure I could not recover, and get my life in order. My drinking was totally out of control, and I had to admit to myself that I could not live without it. I tried to hide it from the children, and stupidly thought they hadn't noticed how bad it was. I started hiding it around the house so that they wouldn't know – under the bed, under the kitchen sink, in cupboards and drawers, anywhere and everywhere. I was also on tranquillizers, which were a necessity. I felt physically and mentally ill, and tired beyond belief. It was at this point that I took an overdose, not to end my life, but to have a rest from responsibilities that I couldn't handle any more. It seemed that however hard I tried to keep my family together, it was an impossible dream, and that that was not the plan life had in store for me. I wanted out – to block it all out, and to wake up and find myself in another world.

I woke up in hospital, with a searing pain in my chest, and connected to a drip. I felt numb – unable to believe that I had really come this far down the line. The enormity of the past horrors and the guilt I felt hung over me like a leaden cloud, obscuring all else. The men in my life had failed me, and in turn I had failed my children.

Although everyone in hospital was very kind and understanding, they could not keep me there longer than a couple of days. A psychiatrist came to see me to establish that I was in a fit mental state to go home. I knew that I wasn't, and that I didn't want to. I must have presented a very forlorn figure, as I can remember his saying that he'd like to put me in his pocket and take me home! If only! He asked me if I would like to be transferred to a psychiatric ward. I agreed, though really had no idea what this would mean. I was buying time.

This was an unbelievably frightening experience. I was put on a drug called Heminevrin, and began to hallucinate wildly. I was terrified of going to sleep for fear of what would transpire in my mind. It was like something out of a Hitchcock movie. I could see myself running across a field, being swooped on by a gigantic eagle, which tore at my brain with its beak and talons – the next minute I was drowning in a bath and, however hard I tried, could not get my head above the water. I must have been screaming, as George, the night nurse, came to my rescue and took me to the day room, where I spent the night drinking cocoa and telling him my life story.

Added to this, there were unearthly screams throughout the nights from another patient who had lost her leg in a car crash, a very large woman who crept up behind me and bellowed 'Hello!' in my ear, which made me leap out of my seat in fright, and other patients I had spoken to on quite a normal basis who would suddenly change personalities altogether. I began to think that perhaps I was going insane, and that I had been put in there for this reason. I kept trying to reassure myself that I was not, though secretly believed it might be possible. Patrick came to see me once while I was there, mainly to gloat I suspect. He took one look at my shaking hands trying to hold a coffee cup, and laughed. He seemed to be pleased, even satisfied, that I had ended up a similar victim of alcohol, and if I were looking for sympathy, it would certainly not be coming from him!

I was there for a fortnight, by which time I definitely wanted to go home. To block out this recent nightmare, I did the only thing I knew that worked – I had a drink, several in fact, until I was back in the old routine.

About a month or so after this event, Patrick was admitted to hospital, after yet another major heart attack, and was in intensive care. I received a phone call from him, asking me if I would bring in some tranquillizers for him to calm him down. He had, by that time, been prescribed the same drug as my own, and apparently they would not give them to him in hospital. I had to refuse, as I could not go against the doctor's decision, and he shouted abuse down the phone at me. The next morning I had a phone call from the hospital to say he had died.

Before he died, Patrick said to me 'I know you've never loved me the way I love you. When I've gone I want you to find someone else and be happy'. I think that his brain had become so addled with alcohol that he couldn't remember the terrifying life he had inflicted on me and my children. I couldn't think of anything to say in reply. He was dying, and any recriminations I might have wanted to air seemed totally pointless.

Guilt is what I felt at his death, thinking that I had somehow caused it, but his actual going brought on a feeling of relief tinged with sadness. He was an intelligent human being, with a good deal of potential, which he had seen fit to put totally to waste. He could have had such a good life, but instead had had no life at all, though I am left with a beautiful daughter, for which I will always thank him. She is tall, slim and blonde, like him.

Mandy, meanwhile, was having a brilliant career in the Navy, having been through university beforehand. She was doing extremely well, had married a naval chap and was living in Plymouth. I saw so little of her, and felt we were growing apart. Her life was so very different from mine – organized and stable, while mine was utter chaos, and I was bitterly ashamed. I desperately wanted to be in touch, but felt I had nothing to offer.

Carrie had also met someone, and was about to have her first baby. She and her husband had separated though, by the time her baby was due, and she wanted me there for the birth. I was extremely nervous at the thought of this – I'd never been on the receiving end before! – but obviously couldn't refuse her. My health was in a rather delicate state by this time, and I just prayed I wouldn't collapse. I'm so glad I was there – it was a wonderful experience, and one that I'll never forget. I held my first grandchild, and thought that no matter what I'd been through, this definitely compensated for it all! It was exactly a year since Patrick had died – one life had been taken, and another given.

Carrie and her husband planned to start again with a new life in Scotland and, on their departure, I felt desperately lonely. Carrie had been my rock, loving and dependable, and without her I saw nothing in my life really beyond a drink and a pill, which kept me going, albeit not on a very reliable basis, and although I thought I had things under control, I obviously hadn't.

I am not the cool enigma that you see
This charade is only planned
To keep you off the scent
And hides a silent plea
If I could only trust, then I would tell
To unburden all this pain
That lies within my heart I'd break the spell
So I'm acting out a play
And hoping that you'll help me
In creating this illusion
While I throw my soul away

I took over Carrie's house in Bideford, a few miles from my present house, thinking that being in a town as opposed to a village, might be better for us all, a bit livelier perhaps. However, although I think it was better for the children I found I was very isolated. Through living with Patrick, and all that had preceded it, I had emerged with virtually no friends to speak of, and I found that my living in a town made no difference. I tried to keep going for the children's sake, but underneath the exterior, was desperately unhappy. I knew that my life was a sham, and that I was totally reliant on alcohol and tranquillizers. To my mind, there really seemed no point in my existence at all.

Carrie, however, eventually split up with her husband and came back home, to my immense relief, but by that time I was too far gone to appreciate it fully. My partner in life was a bottle, to the exclusion of all else, and my days were spent planning how to obtain the money to buy drink for the next day. On one of my 'not so good days' she told me that at the rate I was going, I would lose them all if I didn't get help. I knew that I had to live for their sake, if not for my own, and summoned up the courage to ring Broadreach House Treatment Centre in Plymouth. I had overheard a conversation between a doctor and patient during my stay in the psychiatric ward (isn't it strange that my being there had a purpose after all?) in which Broadreach House had been mentioned. Subconsciously I must have known I would need it one day.

I now felt determined to get myself straight and, you might say, 'get a life'. They accepted me, and I was in treatment for six months, during which time I was totally stripped of all my remaining dignity and most of my pride. It was sheer hell coming off both alcohol and tranquillizers, and I frequently thought I was going to die – there was no turning back though, and I felt compelled to see it through. I kept telling myself the only way I could now go was up. My life certainly could not get worse, so must surely get better. Once the initial physical torture had passed, I discovered that that was a very small part of recovery. Endless therapy sessions followed, in which everyone was encouraged to bare their souls. I found it extremely difficult to open up and talk as, since the age of eight, I had schooled myself into not telling anyone my troubles, and dealing with things myself. Suddenly, to have to reveal all, when I was so ashamed of the failure I had now become, seemed unthinkable. In fact, if it hadn't been for my very persistent and dedicated counsellor, Juliana, who stuck by me, I think I came very close to being asked to leave!

Mandy was wonderful, and came up from Plymouth to fetch me. Both she and Carrie had rallied round immediately with help in getting me there. They were both very concerned about me, and were one hundred per cent behind me. I had to leave Emma alone in the house, which, as she was seventeen, was very worrying, but she did have Carrie close by. I only had to think of Lucy's accommodation for the duration of my stay. Carrie offered to have her, as she and her boyfriend lived just two streets away and had room for her. Lucy was only twelve and I was worried at leaving her for months at a time, but knew she would be all right with Carrie. I had no idea how long I would be, but assumed it would be about eight weeks.

Send me a flower

A rose in the morning

Dew-covered and golden in hue

Send me a rose

With petals of velvet

The spirit of love to renew

Send me a bloom

With a heady perfume

To fill up my senses again

Carry me back

To the child in the garden

Who knew not the meaning of pain

Whilst in the treatment centre, I kept a diary to remind me never to go through this again. The following is an extract from this diary:

26th April 1994 (Tuesday)

Arrived 9.30 a.m. Driven by Mandy. Not too nervous, just uncertain as to what I had ahead of me. Everyone going by first names and very friendly. I shut my eyes before going through the door, and silently offered up a prayer for God to carry me through this and help me to be the person I needed to be.

Saw counsellor and doctor, who took a blood test for liver damage. In the evening saw psychiatrist who was very nice. I have been allotted a 'buddy' to show me the ropes – Mary. Didn't attend any sessions today but am in for it tomorrow. Dosage of Co-

proxamol and Lorazepam reduced by one. Not feeling too bad. The worst they say is yet to come, and that is not coming off the drugs but the therapeutic sessions and write-ups to come.

Everyone smokes in here – twice as much as they did outside. We all meet up, six at a time in the 'Ice Box', the smoking room. We are told to 'share' which means we recount our experiences and talk over group therapy sessions, and anything else that might have happened. Some horrific stories coming out. Had a bath at 10.00 p.m. Back to the 'Ice Box'. See nurse at 11.00 for last medication and bed after. Not too bad a day at all. I feel I'm among friends. After such a long time, it's good to talk to people.

Was given a bag search on coming in. All medicines, razors and perfume taken away. Have been given a folder and file plus pad of paper. Had to write what my impressions were on the first day as I've done here.

Juliana (counsellor) is a very attractive tall blonde with ice-blue eyes. She smokes roll-ups and has a burning red candle on her desk from which she lights the cigarettes.

Everything you own is labelled with your name – down to cups etc. I'm told Juliana is sweetness and light to start with but completely tears you apart later on! She told me that I probably think this is a 'haven' but I'm in for a very hard time emotionally and physically, but most of all emotionally.

I am in a single room to start with and will be put into a room sharing later on. This is because of agoraphobia, which they say will go!

27th April (Wednesday)

3.30 a.m. Can't sleep, every nerve ending is alive. Back's killing me. Feel like pacing up and down.

Up at 6.00 – coffee and down to the 'Ice Box'. Back up to the nurse at 7.00 for medication.

Breakfast 8.00 Exercises in my room. Back up to the nurse for another pill. There is nothing to do until 9.45 except sit in the 'Ice Box' or read the paper which I haven't got. I am in Yellow Group. There are two groups yellow and green. My group are going on a walk this morning (misty rain!) but as it's my first week I don't have to go. Nothing to do all morning but back and forth to the 'Ice Box'!

We had Group Therapy today. I enjoyed it and actually contributed something. Am writing this on the 29th as couldn't write before. Felt too awful and shaking too much. When sitting on a chair, am having to hold on to it to stay on it!

28th April (Thursday)

Had Workshop today. I was terrified. Silent room etc. but more than that, they hit a spot that really I hadn't admitted for years, that I am very shy. I suddenly felt very small and very vulnerable. At the end of the session went into the garden, sat on a bench and had a good cry. I felt totally isolated all of a sudden. No-one here to help me but me. Sat there, thought it through for half an hour and felt better. Got to do this. My first step.

Have just realized (on having been told it's hereditary) that my uncle had a problem with alcohol. Told us that alcoholism is a disease that none of us can be blamed for.

29th April (Friday)

Went to the doctor. My hair is falling out, my skin is dry, my back is worse and I think I have got eczema.

Am told that all the above, apart from the back, are quite normal and that hair loss is due to shock and that it will grow back soon. I certainly hope so!

Group Therapy in the morning. Everybody now knows that I am terrified of silent places with people and that I am having great difficulty in sitting there, because I mentioned it. Got encouragement from several of the group.

Lecture on AIDS. Interesting. All of us here suffering from wind! We're on a high-fibre diet – lots of salads etc.

Evening – I passed out in the Dining Room today. If it hadn't been for Rose hanging on to me I'd have knocked myself out on the table. Everyone rushed round with wet flannels and put my head between my knees until I came to. I gave them all a bit of a fright I think. Have to go to the doctor again.

(29th April again!) Juliana popped up again when I was in the 'Ice Box' and asked me which Maharajah of Jaipur was in my book (I had brought the book in to carry on with, thinking I would have a good deal of spare time in which to write!) I don't know, as my mother didn't mention it. She says she has just been reading a lovely book on India and the fourth Maharajah which she will lend me. Says she is enjoying reading mine!

Much shouting going on today – chaps playing rounders on the lawn! I have never been surrounded by so much love and care in my life. There are some lovely people in here with horrific stories to tell. All like me.

1st May (Sunday)

I'm sure one of the guys next door fell out of bed last night. Hell of a crash about 2.30 a.m.!

Had a good day with Group Therapy in the morning. Rest of the time writing up my Life Story ready to read out tomorrow (very nervous!). Finding it difficult to condense it all. Sunbathing and watching them play rounders. 'Stockport Pete' running like crazy. He really is a character – as wide as he's tall, close cropped hair and bullet-headed! We have everyone here – people fresh out of prison, aristocracy, girls on the game, lesbians, gays – you name it, we've got it. But they truly are a wonderful cross-section of humanity, and I feel privileged to know them. Monique (prostitute) couldn't hack it and left today. Not enough money in here!

2nd May (Monday)

I did my Life Story today. Had to read it out in front of everyone (thirty-six residents). Absolutely ghastly! I shook so that I had to put the paper down on my knees to keep it still. Got hugs from everyone at the end. Thank God that's over. It's been a beautiful day here weather-wise and I've been in the garden doing my Life Story for most of it.

3rd May (Tuesday)

I woke in complete panic this morning at 7.00 wondering where I was. On opening my eyes, I don't think it took me long to realize. Whilst doing TD's (Therapeutic Duties) fainted again in the Dining Room. Sat down with everyone concerned as usual, went outside after half an hour with Eileen to have a cigarette and collapsed again against Martin (lovely looking, very quiet London guy). They sent me to bed. Felt really dreadful. On only half a pill twice a day.

4th May (Wednesday)

A very emotional group in the morning. One of the girls recounted her story of being raped by seven men. I could relate to that with my own rape experience at fifteen. I left the group feeling very sad.

5th May (Thursday)

Someone who was here a couple of years ago died today from a drug overdose. Half the house was crying. We had a House Group about it to express how we felt. Sat through it feeling nothing, but when Rose and I got outside both of us cried, thinking 'there but for the grace of God', and of all the loved ones we would leave behind. We collapsed in each other's arms.

6th May (Friday)

Dentist in the morning and nice to get out for a bit. Felt very odd. Mohammed gave a really wonderful lecture this afternoon. Such a gentle man. He was here when I came and I've found him easy to talk to, and more near my age than most! The majority are quite young, though age is immaterial.

This is the last entry in my diary.

CHAPTER 11

I gave up writing the diary in the end, as I just had too much work to do, writing out every wrong thing I had ever done and every experience I had been through, which took up a considerable amount of paper!

This was altogether a very hard time, in which I had to face up to the disaster my life now was. To repair shattered illusions and non-existent self-esteem was the job of the counsellors and was a mammoth task, and many would return later, or perhaps not at all, not being ready to face this life-shattering experience. I knew that I had lived more than half my life, and that if I wanted to live the rest, I had to go through this. Time was running out, and there was nowhere to hide. Exposure seemed the only available route. It was a very tough and humbling experience, and one that I would not wish ever to go through again.

They definitely saved my life, and put me back on track. I was there for three months, then went on to secondary care in Bristol for another three months – after which I had definitely had enough, and didn't think they could do anything more for me. There was much protesting from the counsellors with regard to my going, as they were adamant that I needed further therapy. However, I was also adamant that I did not!

Today's the day my life begins
When dormant plans are formed
Ideas and dreams made into schemes
And thoughts to act upon
If I put off what I can do I'll never know the truth
And live my life in ignorance
Spent longing for my youth
Sealed in the corners of my mind
Are places not yet seen
Exotic countries beckon me
With dreams that might have been
They're not as far as one might think
If I could just decide
To open up the universe
And bring its light inside
Ask strength and love to hold my hand
And take me on a trip
With light and hope a net to spread
Perchance that I should slip

To attempt to portray the depth of my emotions throughout a life of constant trauma would be impossible. Not that I find it impossible to relive the feelings, rather that words alone are not sufficient to express the loneliness, pain and despair I have frequently felt – I suppose, with time, I have learned to quash my feelings in order to survive – to shake off any emotion that would pull me down, and which could possibly stifle my reasoning. If I have felt I am in danger of losing control, I change channels, like a television set, and employ 'tunnel vision' to overcome a problem!

I must admit that at the end of all this, I made a list of all the people and events that had hurt me, and came to the conclusion that it was no wonder I had emerged the worse for wear! Seeing it all laid out in black and white put things into perspective for me. Although we were told in therapy that we were not the victims, but that other people, family and friends were on the receiving end, I think that one's own life has to be taken into account, and that it probably ends up being six of one and half a dozen of the other – one resulting in the other. I am not making excuses, however, for my behaviour, as I fully realize what a worrying and frightening nightmare I must have become to live with and to know, for the ones I love dearly, and who love me. If it had not been for Carrie initially jolting me into reality, I really don't think I would have survived, or if I had I would have lost my children. Also there was the fact that if I went, my children would have been left without their mother – I couldn't do this to them after all they had been through, and all we meant to each other. Although it seems very dark at the time, and that no-one understands, there is always an answer, and the motto is 'never give up'!

Only a few months after I arrived home, my father died. He

had been such a strong, well-built man, and always there for me. To see him gradually deteriorating was very sad. However, he lived to the ripe old age of ninety-one, a good innings. I think after having lost my mother, he just had nothing left to live for, and in fact admitted that he'd had enough, and didn't want to be around any more. My having been away for so long must have made him feel even lonelier, as I had been in close contact with him most days. He would walk over to see me from Appledore right up into his late eighties!

His last Christmas was a very sad one. I had been in touch with the care home where he lived to arrange his visit to us for Christmas and had arranged his room etc. for the couple of days of his stay. He arrived on the doorstep with a suitcase full of most of his things, expecting to stay indefinitely. It was a dreadful time in which I had to try to get through to him that he was only there for the two days of Christmas and not for good. He was so confused and upset, and it broke my heart to see it. By this time he really didn't know where he was or what was happening to him, and we all felt so helpless in the face of this obvious decline.

I was so proud of Mandy when she stood up in church in her naval uniform and recited 'Devon Man' for him at his funeral. He too, being a lover of the sea, I'm sure appreciated it.

DEVON MAN

Give him a pipe and a book of the sea
His favourite spaniel curled up on his knee

Give him a day in the frost and sun

His dog at his heel, his hand on his gun

Give him the waves and the wind and wet

With muscle a-strain at a fisherman's net

Give him a horse and a 'View Halloo!'

When scent is keen and the hounds run true

You'll grant his hopes this side of heaven

If it's country life – and the country's Devon.

Marjorie Leslie

On his going I suddenly felt very alone – that I had no-one to turn to any more, and that I was the one my family would be turning to in the future. I was no longer the 'child'; there was no-one to look up to or seek advice from. My childhood had finally gone.

I was the head of the family. The thought of it sent a feeling of panic through me. I just hoped that I could be strong enough to cope. I could no longer drown my sorrows with a drink or a pill, or find courage from a bottle, and with my parents gone there were no crutches of any sort. However, all four of my daughters had been positively behind me up to now, and I had no reason to suppose they would now falter in this. To have them all still supporting me after the agonies I must have put them through was nothing short of a miracle, and I felt very honoured that they should still feel the same.

For a time I felt very lost and alone, and wondered where

my life was going – I couldn't really see any future. Although I was now alcohol and drug free, this alone was obviously not sufficient to fill the empty days that lay ahead. My outlook on life changed and I thought that after having been so close to death and having survived, that there must after all be a God who cared, and that perhaps there was indeed a reason behind it all.

I am your heartbeat steady, strong
I am the line twixt right and wrong
I am the answer when you call
I am the writing on the wall
I am the voice to quell your fear
When days of paradise draw near
I am the hand to guide you through
To lift you up to life anew
I am the love that's always been
That life-enhancing go-between
I am the comfort in the dark
The fire behind the lighted spark
I am the star that draws you home
And guides your footsteps when you roam
I am your true self – heed my word
For always shall my voice be heard
I am the strength behind the sword
I am the Lord

I became interested in spiritual healing, and through a friend of Carrie's, found Hazel. After several weekly sessions with her my faith in myself, and in God, were restored and I emerged feeling strong, young and alive. She has been instrumental in giving me back my strength, and the belief in myself that I thought I had lost, and without whose encouragement I would not have written this book. She was amazingly accurate in revealing past experiences and her assessment of my character and those around me, and I learnt a great deal from her – my view of the world changed and I began to see people in a different light, with a more charitable approach.

In a 'past life' regression she revealed that I am afraid of water (very true), and proceeded to explain that she could see me sliding down the slippery deck of a sixteenth-century sailing ship, floundering in heavy seas and rapidly keeling over, trying to cling on to the halyards to stop myself from being swallowed by the waves. I had voluminous skirts, which, being saturated and heavy with sea water, were dragging me down. Whether I did actually drown I am not sure, but I know that I have always had a deep fear of water, finding in the hidden depths of lakes and rivers a definite sense of menace and foreboding. If swimming in a pool or the sea and my feet no longer touch the bottom I immediately panic.

In another life I had apparently had my head shaved to make me look unattractive, and this one I rather like – Hazel could see me as an Egyptian high priestess coming down some palace steps wearing a long flowing turquoise gown trimmed with silver! She also said that I could 'see beyond', meaning I think that I know the outcome of a series of events before the events have taken place, which is often quite true, though whether I reach the conclusion by logical steps or intuition I'm not too sure. It can, however, apply to years of events and the ultimate conclusion! Also the truth behind the lie!

I'm much more astute now, and take more time to listen than I used to. I have an idea for the future that hopefully one day I can put into practice – a retreat for people who need to acclimatize after having been through a treatment centre – to experience a touch of luxury, plus some form of training, giving them something to aim for in the future. To be sent straight out into the outside world with no plan, apart from never having a drink or a drug again, I consider to be a very bleak prospect, and one that I'm sure is enough to turn one back along the same road in many cases. However, as this particular project would undoubtedly run into costs of millions I can't really see it materializing! I've no doubt someone, with readily available finances, will beat me to it and put the plan into action in the future.

There's no nightmare to come home to any more
No secrets I've kept locked behind the door
My brain is free to think again
My life is for the taking
I've risen like a phoenix from the floor
The guilt and pain I've harboured for so long

Are now a distant memory, long gone

I feel young, alive and free

With a future I can see

In my heart, once dead and leaden, there's a song

If you'd told me this three years ago today

I'd have told you there's too high a price to pay

I did not have the courage

Or the strength with which to face it

And I'd given up on God and ceased to pray

Love, strength, and faith are priceless gifts

Revered since time began

These gathered in, a spirit lifts

So catch them if you can

I began to think a lot about my brother Tim, and realized that I really had no idea where he had been buried. I imagined it was in the churchyard of my childhood Sunday school. I talked it over with Mandy, and she offered to take me to Taunton to see if we could find him. She came up from Plymouth one Sunday in December and we set off.

To be back in Taunton, the town where I was born, filled me with nostalgia. It was a lovely feeling, and we sought out my old house, where I had spent the first twelve years of my life, and my grandparents' house next door. It was amazing to find that, apart from most of the surrounding trees having been cut down, and the hedge round my grandparents' house also having gone, nothing else had changed, and I was back to being six years old, coming up the path with tadpoles in a jam-jar to show my mother!

We set off to find the church. It was a very old and pretty church, with a lovely litch gate. On our approach an elderly, grey-haired lady walked towards us, with a firm and sprightly step. She looked at me, held my gaze then looked away. By the time she had gone, I realized who she was – I'm almost sure she was my old headmistress! It would appear that, by the way she had looked at me, there had been a spark of recognition, although I doubt that she remembered where she knew me from.

My old Sunday school was where it had always been, and brought back so many memories. It was in a separate hall to the left of the main church, and Mandy and I went over to investigate. It was almost as I had left it. The children's paintings on the walls and the little wooden chairs encircling low, round tables, that hadn't moved their location in nearly fifty years! The hall was full of people and buzzing with life – everyone chattering avidly to the clink of teacups. A meeting of some sort had just taken place and we were immediately asked if we'd like a cup of tea. It was all very welcoming and warm. I remarked on how little things had changed since I was five years old, and people smiled in agreement.

We walked towards the church to the strains of 'O Worship the King' coming from within, and waited outside until the service had finished. We met the church warden, who on receipt of our request, set off to look through the record books to trace Tim's burial. He emerged triumphant with the book in his hand about ten minutes later, and took us through the churchyard to locate the grave. There was nothing there, nothing at all to mark the place. No headstone – nothing. I can't explain how sad I felt at this discovery. Tim had been so young and alive, so to find his going had not even been marked was a tragedy. I suppose there had been no money available to do anything, and I vowed there and then that he should not continue to be neglected, and that I would come here whenever I could.

A few months later, I wrote to the church warden to ask if it would be possible to erect some form of plaque or headstone, and to plant a rose bush. He replied that he would have to obtain permission and would get in touch. For several months I heard nothing, and decided to ring and find out what had happened. I was very sad to learn that he had died just a month before my call. He was such a kind man and not at all old.

My interest in my mother's background was rekindled, and I set out to explore the family history. During the ensuing months I became engrossed in finding out more about the Leslie family.

I was under the impression (from my mother) that the family could only be traced back as far as Mary, Queen of Scots, but I have now found out, as I have previously stated, that the Leslies go right back to 1070, when Bartholomew de Lesley married Princess Beatrix, the sister of King Malcolm III Canmore of Scotland. He was extremely capable and physically strong, and the king made him Commander of Edinburgh Castle.

My mother also told me that the motto was bestowed on the Leslies when Mary, Queen of Scots was crossing from the mainland of Scotland to the Isle of Skye – she fell overboard and a Leslie took off his belt and told her to 'grip fast' in order to pull her to safety. However, I discovered from the late Chief of Clan Leslie, Ian Malcolm Leslie, Lord Rothes (pronounced Rothez), a different version, originating much earlier in the eleventh century when Bartholomew and Queen Margaret of Scotland were making a journey. One of the chamberlain's tasks was to transport his mistress, who rode side-saddle, 'pillion', on a small pad behind his saddle, and she would hold on to the stout belt around his waist, the badge of office for a chamberlain. On one occasion when, with the queen riding pillion, they were crossing a burn in full flood, the horse stumbled and Bartholomew, thinking the queen might fall off, cried 'Grip fast!' and she replied in alarm 'Gin the buckle bide?' (Will the buckle hold?). They reached the far bank safely but were so shaken by the incident that 'Grip fast' became their motto and Bartholomew added two more buckles to his belt for added security.

Bartholomew's son, Malcolm, was knighted by King David, the Leslie lands being granted him by Royal Charter. This charter is one of the oldest surviving land charters in Aberdeenshire. Further down the line, in the fourteenth century John, son of Andrew the 6th Lord Leslie, was created Earl of Rothes, and the 22nd Earl of Rothes is chief of Clan Leslie today.

John Leslie Bishop of Ross, born in 1526, became the most loyal of all the supporters of Mary, Queen of Scots, and wrote *The History of Scotland* for her in the Scottish vernacular. Included in Scotland's stormy history was the murder of David Beaton, Cardinal Archbishop of St Andrews, in 1546. He was murdered in his palace and this, in fact, was thought to be a private Leslie vendetta, though the Leslie in question was later acquitted.

As I mentioned before, Leslie House in Fife still stands, though it was sold in 1919, and is now the property of the Church of Scotland. The last family of Leslies to live in Leslie House were the late 21st Earl of Rothes, Ian Leslie, his parents and grandparents. There are branches of the family all over the world, many families descending from the barons of Balquain, this being the most prolific line, in particular from the third baron, Andrew. Many families descend from Andrew among them the Earls of Leven, the Lords Newark, the Leslies of Pitcaple, Kininvie, Iden and Cults and in Ireland the Leslies of Kincraigie, Glaslough and Tarbert, the Lords Leslie in Russia, the Counts Leslie in France and the Holy Roman Empire. From these and other branches Leslies spread from Scotland all over the world, many going to the United States and Canada, starting in the eighteenth century and continuing into the nineteenth.

There is a connection with the Leslies of Glaslough and the Churchill family. Sir John Leslie of Castle Leslie, Glaslough, married Leonie, one of the three beautiful Jerome sisters of

New York. Her sister, Jennie, married Lord Randolph Churchill and their son, Winston, often visited his Leslie aunt and uncle at Glaslough. The castle was originally built by the 'Fighting Bishop' two-and-a-quarter centuries earlier, and was completely rebuilt by Sir John in the 1870s. He was a great admirer of Italian art and architecture, and the beautiful rooms and Italianate cloister reflect this. It overlooks Glaslough (the Green Lake) and is surrounded by landscaped grounds. Sir John, unlike his great-grandfather, strongly supported Union with Britain, which for a while caused strained relations with his nephew Winston Churchill, who, as an MP, equally strongly supported Home Rule for Ireland.

My great-grandfather Sheppard John Leslie, established the family firm of solicitors, and his son Franklin Marston Leslie, my grandfather, carried on in the family business in Calcutta, where he met and married my grandmother, and where my mother was born. On speaking to the late earl, he asked me how I felt about finding my family, and I replied 'At last I know who I am. I feel I've come home!' and he replied 'Good, I'm glad'. I now also know why my mother took such pains to steer me on the course she did, although at the time it made no sense to me at all. I'm so glad she persevered, as without her stories perhaps I would not have known about my really quite adventurous family at all.

Carrie and I were passing a shop window one day recently, and noticed a framed copy of the *New York Times* in which it gave the first report on the disaster of the sinking of the *Titanic*. On looking down the list of survivors, we were thrilled to see the Countess of Rothes – the late Earl's grandmother. Her name was Noel (Lucy Noel Martha) and she married Norman Evelyn Leslie, 19th Earl of Rothes in 1900, when only sixteen years old. They lived in Scotland in the ancestral home of the Earls of Rothes at Leslie House in Fife. She boarded the ship in Southampton, accompanied by her cousin and her personal maid, and was given cabin 77 on 'C' Deck. They sailed for New York on 10 April 1912. An account of this has been written by her grandson Ian, 21st Earl of Rothes, a copy of which he was kind enough to send me and I quote:

'They had retired early on the night of the disaster, and were awakened by a slight shock at 11.45 p.m. and noticed that the engines had stopped. On enquiring from their cabin steward they were told that the ship had been in collision with some ice. Wanting to see an iceberg, they went up on deck but saw no sign of the iceberg, only the deck covered in ice. On their way back to their cabin they met the Purser, who told them to put on some warm clothing and return to 'A' Deck.

In her statement for the official inquiry, made later to the British Vice-Consul in Los Angeles, Noel states that at no time was there any sign of panic. She relates how they returned to 'A' Deck where several people had already congregated, they were instructed by the Captain to get into Lifeboat No. 8 with several other women and children, a cook, a steward and an Able Seaman Jones in charge. They were told to row over to a ship whose lights were visible not far away and then the seaman was to return for more passengers. There was some discussion as to whether they should go back to take more people in their boat but the majority were afraid that the suction might take them down with it, so it was decided to row over to the ship. In a completely matter of fact way Noel goes on to relate how she volunteered to take the tiller so that A/B Jones could row, the cook and steward not being seamen were not able to help. Later she gave the tiller to her cousin and herself rowed for the rest of the night. After several very cold hours, as dawn was breaking, they were picked up by the *Carpathia*. Although never proved, it seems the lights they had seen originally were from another vessel whose identity was never discovered but which never saw them and eventually turned away. This meant they rowed a long way in the wrong direction before sighting the *Carpathia*.

A/B Jones's version of what happened, as reported in the press, is similar if more dramatic. In spite of the terrible predicament in which he suddenly found himself he is reported as having maintained a cheerful and encouraging disposition throughout. As a seaman of some years' experience, the sea itself would not have alarmed him but suddenly to be in command of a lifeboat full of cold and terrified women with no help whatsoever must have been a terrifying experience. To find Noel with some knowledge of boats (her husband had a yacht) must have been a tremendous relief since the cook and steward, the only other men in the boat, were completely ignorant.

The *Daily Telegraph* of 22nd April 1912, reported as follows:

The Countess of Rothes is now in the Ritz-Carton hotel, New York under the care of a physician. I learn that it is not so much exposure which has made her ill as the effects of her hard labour in pulling at the oars. Her boat was undermanned... One able-bodied seaman (Jones), who shipped aboard the *Titanic* when she left Southampton, is tired and a little listless and subdued from the things he lived through last Monday, but his eyes light up and his speech becomes animated when you ask him what part the women played in the trying hours after the *Titanic* sank. "There was a woman in my boat as was a woman" he told the *Daily Telegraph* representative yesterday. "She was the Countess of Rothes. I was one of those ordered to man the boats, and my place was in No. 8 lifeboat. There were thirty-five of us in that boat, but I had to row, and I wanted someone at the tiller. When I saw the way she was carrying herself, and heard the quiet, determined way she spoke to the others, I knew she was more of a man than any we had aboard, and I put her in command. I put her at the tiller, and she was at the tiller when the *Carpathia* came along five hours later. And there was another woman on board who was strong in the work we had to do. She was at the oar with me, and though I never learned her name she was helping every minute [Noel's cousin?]. It was she who suggested we should sing. "Sing" you say, I should think we did! It kept up our spirits. We sang as we rowed, all of us, starting with "Pull for the Shore" and we were still singing when we saw the lights of the *Carpathia*. Then we stopped singing and prayed.

The evidence of the Official Inquiry confirms A/B Jones's story, except that other accounts (including Noel's) say Noel gave the tiller to Gladys Cherry (her cousin) and it was she (Noel) who rowed all night.

Noel fainted from exhaustion as she was hoisted on to the *Carpathia* but once she had recovered she devoted herself to the welfare of the other survivors, particularly the steerage women and children. Her Victorian upbringing would have stood her in good stead at this time and she busied herself making clothes for the children and comforting the many widows and those who had lost loved ones.

The Grove newspaper reported:

All the women who were in the boats spoke with great admiration and gratitude of Lady Rothes, who rowed all night in one of the boats, and devoted herself the whole time she was on the *Carpathia* to the care of the steerage women and children. She helped to make clothes for the babies and became known among the crew as "The Plucky Little Countess".

It took the *Carpathia* four days to reach New York, where Noel's husband was waiting to meet her. Noel left Leslie House in April with auburn hair and returned four months later with completely white hair.

Noel never spoke of her experience afterwards, but she wrote to her parents when she was still aboard the *Carpathia* which gives some insight into the horrors of that night, telling how she cared for a woman who had lost seven of her eight children and her husband; a Hungarian woman who went berserk thinking she had lost her tiny baby, which later was found; the French lady who was frantic and could not be left alone for fear she would kill herself and a young Spanish girl, on her honeymoon, whose husband had put her in Noel's arms and begged Noel to look after her. The husband stayed on board and perished, the girl spoke no English and knew only one person in the whole of America.

Noel says in her letter:

"But oh! the horror of it all can never be told, and those fearful cries as she sank will never go out of my head and I am one of the lucky ones".

She was indeed one of the lucky ones, since she was one of the few who did not lose a loved one that night. Of just over 700 survivors, the great majority were women and children most of whom would have lost a husband or father.

A/B Jones did not go back to sea after the tragedy, but retired to a Seaman's Home in Southampton. He stayed in touch with Noel for the rest of his life. He obtained the actual brass number "8" from the lifeboat when it was broken up and he mounted it on a small wooden plaque which he presented to my grandmother. We still have the plaque and his letter in our possession. The only other memento we have is the pearl necklace she was wearing, this was a necklace of Scottish freshwater pearls given to her by her husband on her wedding, which she wore all the time. Her other jewellery was locked away in the safe in the Purser's office and was lost with the ship.

The Paris edition of the New York Herald published a poem dedicated to Noel as follows:

(It will be remembered that the Countess of Rothes, who is an expert oarswoman, took charge of one of the lifeboats of the *Titanic*. The entire management of the boat fell to her, none of the men in it having any expert knowledge of seamanship or of the art of rowing.)

It is rather more a jingle than a rhyme
The metre may be wrong
For the meaning of the song
Is somehow much more precious than the time
Being all about the lady
At the tiller of the boat
The boat the little lady
Kept afloat
All aboard the boat were fearful of the cold
Their voices seemed so weak
When they did their best to speak
That soon they only did as they were told
By the clear-voiced little lady

At the tiller of the boat
The boat the gentle lady
Kept afloat
The women had to pull the boat in turn
The cold was felt no more
As each struggled with an oar
And all that could not row were made to learn
By the quiet little lady
At the tiller of the boat
The boat the noble lady
Kept afloat
She worked a living miracle on board
She tempted them to sing
Just a snatch of anything
Till they lifted up their hearts unto the Lord
With the gallant little lady
At the tiller of the boat
The boat the loyal lady
Kept afloat
Any time at all will do to shout
In honour of her name
For her light is steady flame
And many could not bear to do without
The splendid little lady
The good angel of the boat
Through her, who knows how many
Kept afloat?'

Noel is portrayed in the film *Titanic* as the Countess of Ross, a title which died out early on in the family. This is rather a feeble representation of her and certainly does not do her justice!

This has all been a fascinating discovery, and I am increasingly in touch with family members all over the world as a result. My aim now is to go to India to try to recapture some of the splendour of my mother's life there, and to establish whether the house is still standing. I think perhaps I should keep an account of my trip, as my grandmother had done before me. Who knows what the future holds, but I'm sure it will be full of surprises. I firmly believe that life is what you make it – and I'll try to make it interesting. It is a wonderful feeling to be free.

I owe my children so much through all this, for their unfailing love, faith and support, which I consider myself so very lucky to have. I am whole again, with no brittle veneer, and hopefully the traumas I have experienced will enable me to help others also to come through and win.

I now realize how very precious life is, and am far more aware of my own mortality. Being the product of our experiences, it would be futile to try to change that, or to wish we were someone else! Suffering is part of our lives and enhances our perception of other people in the process. We grow stronger because of it, and our understanding of each other deepens through our own experiences. As we only have one chance to make a go of it in our individual forms, it would seem sensible to live it to the full, in as many aspects as possible, and not to waste the tools we have been given.

Also, it is important to know who we are, and to harness, and to put to constructive use, whatever talents we have at our disposal – and we all have them if we look. Not to miss opportunities because we are too scared to try, but to do it anyway. Shut your eyes, take a deep breath, and 'go for it'! The feeling of achievement afterwards is well worth the fear. The braver you get, the more rewarding and fulfilling life can be. All the power you need is within you, and everyone has the potential to improve their life and to be happy – it's just a question of looking inwards for the answer. Don't look back on your life in years to come, and wish you had had the courage to change it; do it now, whatever that change may be.

River of light carry me on to the sea
Spread your light and let it shine
On mortals such as me
Lift me up and let me float
On seas of hope and love
Let me know the state of mind
That I've been dreaming of
Push, cajole me, then enfold me
Be there when I fall
Come with outstretched arms to greet me
In every port of call

Leslie family home, 10 Queen's Park Ballygunge Calcutta.

Summer Bungalow - 'Redlands', Shillong.

Grandfather Leslie, my mother and 'Skittles' Calcutta India

My grandfather, Lt. Col. Franklin Marston Leslie. Painting by A.E Harris

Passage to India. My mother on board ship

The Leslie horses - Black Douglas, The Siren, Challenger, Redland, Redwing and Shrapnell

Leslie House, Fife - Home of the Earls of Rothes.

Ballinbreich Castle on the river Tay.

Leslie Castle, Glaslough Co. Monaghan. Taken from a drawing

Balgonie Castle, Fife, on the banks of the river Leven.

Leslie Castle, Aberdeenshire before restoration.

Leslie Castle after restoration, from a drawing by Michael Mann.

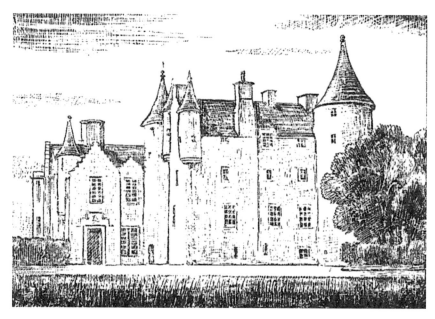

Pitcaple Castle, taken from a drawing - A still occupied Leslie Castle.

EPILOGUE

Looking back on my own personal experience, I have come to the conclusion that I do not consider alcoholism/addiction to be a disease. Being addicted to alcohol in itself is not a disease, though one can obviously become diseased through the prolonged use of alcohol and drugs, as the toll they take is devastating to both mind and body, ending frequently in death. Addiction is a compulsion to ply the mind and body with relief from stress, or to create a feeling of exhilaration and euphoria. An escape from the pressures of reality. A craving which has to be satisfied.

Addiction is a comfort, an easing of mental anguish, boredom or, perhaps for some, starts as just an experiment to try a new sensation. If repeated often it becomes a 'habit', and the body will then have got used to receiving this shot of brain-altering substance. In a short space of time the body will expect this substance and will react violently if it does not receive it. The user becomes 'hooked' and forced into 'injecting' the substance into the bloodstream to stave off the tremors and altered bodily functions, which have arisen due to the lack of it.

With hindsight I can see that it took the gradual increasing of my intake of alcohol to reach that pinnacle of a 'high' sensation, and the more I took the shorter that period lasted. The result in the end was feeling sick and ill most of the time. This condition is self-inflicted, which is why it is not, in my opinion, a disease in the accepted sense of the word. The onset of alcoholism/drug addiction is entirely the responsibility of the perpetrator, who chooses to do this. It starts out as a psychological condition, culminating in both psychological and physical symptoms. One can become diseased in time through repeated and excessive use of a chosen substance, but at the onset of addiction one is not. It still, however, remains 'addiction'. As soon as the user feels he has to have that substance to enable him to function, he is addicted.

There are numerous addictions – chocolate, shopping, food, sex, gambling, and the equally dangerous one of prescribed drugs such as tranquillizers, all of which are instruments for feeling good or a craving for what does not appear to come naturally. Alcoholism can start by taking a drink before an interview or before making a speech to give you courage. It then perhaps becomes necessary to have the odd drink during the day just to 'lift the spirits a bit'. This then snowballs into the necessity for having a drink before even leaving the house in the morning – because you don't feel 'right' and do not have the courage to go out without it. You then start hiding it because guilt is now paramount, and you don't want family and friends to know just how much you are actually drinking. You become terrified that they will find the bottle under the kitchen sink or under the mattress or in the wardrobe. Even more terrifying is the thought that they may find it and pour it down the drain! You become very adept at hiding it and lie quite readily and easily if challenged on the subject. You are now a full-blown alcoholic and embarking on a road to complete self-destruction.

Your mind is in turmoil. You know what you are doing is wrong, yet you cannot stop. You are a prisoner, and the bottle/drug of choice your ever-present jailer. The hurt that you have suffered in the past, far from being obliterated, is now all-enveloping. And added to this is the terrible feeling of guilt and the knowledge that you are now hurting the people you love and who love you. You now have two choices – death or seeking help.

You already feel like death, so it would seem to be the easy way out. But what about the people you will leave behind, not to mention the legacy of failure? You think that perhaps this would be a relief to the people who are left, but on further consideration it would actually seem to be very selfish. You are depriving them of the beautiful person that you really are, and the happiness and pleasure that your being a part of their lives gives to them. The time has come for you to find that person again. You are a good person at heart, not this helpless, addicted, pathetic and objectionable substitute for a human being.

Professional help is a must, and to use your own willpower is not, in almost all cases, enough. You need time and above all exclusion from family and friends to be able to identify what it was that started your craving for oblivion in the first place. This time of regression and reflection is desperately important and one that should not be taken lightly. To be able to unburden childhood anxieties and fears, traumatic incidents that have shaped your life and your character is all-important in making you whole again. To be able to talk to someone who will not judge your actions, both past and present, is instrumental in rebuilding a shattered spirit. No-one can touch your soul, but your spirit can be damaged beyond endurance. What lies ahead is not easy and there are times that would seem to be too difficult to tackle – things that are too painful to say – but you must speak of them. It is only when you are free of concealing the hurt that you will be able to look forward to the future instead of being tethered and weighed down by the past. If these feelings are not aired they will draw you back to the bottle in a very short space of time!

Our past experiences make us the people we are now. It is only by experiencing hurt and pain that our characters grow in strength and are able to develop, and to appreciate and empathize with the hurt in others. The older we get, the wiser we supposedly become. Therefore, use the wisdom you know to be there and the courage to back it up. Seek help.

I am also of the opinion that once you have declared yourself an 'alcoholic' you are not one for life. I believe that once the compulsive drinking has stopped, the demons have been laid to rest and your body and mind are whole again, life can start afresh. I believe it is detrimental to one's recovery to stay rooted in the past and to keep the addiction alive by continually attending AA meetings and mixing in the company of people with a similar background, and at each meeting declaring yourself an 'alcoholic', your conversation and common bond being that of alcohol and/or drugs. This I consider to be an unhealthy approach to a 'new' life. I appreciate that for some this might be the only way to stay 'clean', but for the majority I do not think this is so. To base your whole life on concentrating on never having another drink I believe is more likely to encourage 'relapse' than concentrating on a new and interesting future.

Fear is the strongest deterrent for keeping one on the straight and narrow. I have a complete horror of ever finding myself in the terrifying situation again – where life is so totally out of control and there is no future apart from the next drink. One's whole identity is swimming and drowning in alcohol. To feel desperate, unloved, unwanted, without purpose, suicidal, incarcerated in a liquid haze is the ultimate of misery. I had no personality. I did not know who I was or even how strong a character I possibly had. My past, and the drowning of it in a bottle, had taken away my true identity. I knew that I was not a 'bad' person but that person was so lost and buried as to seem beyond redemption. The fear of ever reaching such a state of degradation again is enough to keep me looking forward.

I have written this book in the hope that it will help anyone who is going through, or has been through, the agonies of alcoholism to realize that there is life after this living hell, and that life is good.

'One day at a time' is a good philosophy to begin with, but life is more than one day. Successful businessmen and women, entrepreneurs and adventurers of today did not get where they are by thinking 'one day at a time'! They thought ahead, dreamed and planned, and that is what life is all about. Making one's dreams come true! You can do it, because I have.

My child
When you are weeping
My shoulder is there for you
When you are laughing I shall laugh with you
When you are afraid I shall comfort you
In moments of joy
I shall rejoice with you
When you are in doubt
I shall endeavour to guide you
To my last breath
I shall be there for you
And no matter what you do
I shall always love you.

EMMA'S DIARY

An incredible journey
(To reach the 'Eternal Snows' of the Himalayas)

In 1891 two young women set out on a truly remarkable
journey on horseback, with just their syces as 'protection'
against all possible unforeseen dangers – my intrepid
grandmother Emma Leslie and her equally fearless
friend Miss Jacob.

Extracts from my grandmother's diary

> Ride up the Happy Valley
>   of the Thelum
>   from Murree.
>
> Monday. 16th Septr '91.
> We started punctually. Miss
> Jacob & I, meeting above the
> Murree Post Office. She on her
> own white horse — while I was
> obliged to start in a dandy for the
> first 12 miles. having posted
> my horse "Coraith" (an arab,)
> & another horse "Laddie" for
> Miss Jacob & me. The road
> was in good condition, being
> the cart-road used by every
> one now bound for Kashmir,
> the old bridle path leaving

or melons or woods keep
up a perfect kaleidoscope
effect. at one time we will
look both up & down the
river for a good distance
& at each end there was
background of hills some
with stray patches of snow
making a lovely picture
then a turn would bring
Serinagur fort into the
background making
quite another view in the
shifting scene.
At last we got clear of
the town by turning at
right angles up a nullah
a mooring on the banks of

what is called the Chenaar
Bagh — the Bagh being
formed by groves of these
beautiful trees, with their
enormous trunks standing
up straight & tall with
their lovely heavy foliage
casting a deep shade on
the glade of grass under
them where numbers of
tents of all sizes, were
pitched: a good number
of boats were moored
along here but we found
a nice quiet & private
place for ourselves — after
which we went for a walk
first of course to the Post

RIDE UP THE HAPPY VALLEY OF THE JHELUM FROM MURREE

By Emma Helen Leslie

Monday 14th September 1891

We started punctually Miss Jacob and I, meeting above the Murree Post Office, she on her own white horse – while I was obliged to start in a dandy for the first 12 miles, having posted my horse 'Coraitn' (an arab) and our other horse 'Laddie' for Miss Jacob's use. The road was in good condition, being the cart road used by everyone now bound for Kashmir, the old bridle path having been discarded as in every way unsuitable. The hills were all round us, covered with pines and oak and many small shrubs of various kinds looking very fresh and green but monotonous in their grandeur. We reached Rawat Rest House to find that two gentlemen had just left, having used it the previous night; the Chowkidar was most attentive in opening the house and attending to all our wants – the posted horses were nowhere to be found, but after a great deal of enquiry we heard that they had passed, going on to a village 2¼ miles away – fortunately our servant in the 'Ekkah' containing our bedding had the sense to send them back to us – no sooner did my jampanees see them than

191

they asked to be allowed to go, so we emptied the contents of our tiffin bucket into the Bungalow plates and cups and let them go, taking back some exquisite grass and enormous cones I had gathered on the road – they had not left more than a quarter of an hour, when on beginning our cold breakfast we discovered there were no knives and forks to be found, so were reduced to using our never-to-be-despised fingers – and good use we made of them! Also of a miniature pen-knife which had never before been in such request.

We thought of waiting till 4 p.m. before continuing our ride, but by 12 o'clock it became cloudy and cool, a few drops of rain falling, deluding us into thinking that the clouds would continue heavy – we started on the 16 mile march to Kohallah. Half an hour after our start the sun came out in all its glory and mid-day heat, not by any means appreciated by us, especially as our road was all on the decline, we having to drop from 7,500 ft. to 2,000 in the 26 miles from Murree: this portion was most prosaic, the sun stinging – the glare bad – and the one object being to get down as quickly as possible to the River Jhelum which (we were told) lay in the bottom of the valley. We strained our eyes in vain to catch sight of the river till 3 o'clock and then the sight rejoiced our eyes tho' it was only a tiny gleam far down below us – however, we brightened over the peep we got tho' we were passing through a belt of pine trees, charred and dead from a recent fire, looking so forlorn, for a mile and a half, when we noticed how the trees were greener again, only here and there where the ambitious flames had reached, scorching what they touched: it must have been a grand sight when alight, the resinous nature of the pines must have made such a fierce and lurid light.

And so we went on and on, down, down, down, at a steady walk and at last reached the Jhelum, the road turning and joining the river's course – how refreshing it was! The cool sound of the splash of the spray as the river rushed past huge boulders was a perfectly delicious sound to us who were hot, so dusty and thirsty, vowing internally to avoid afternoon marches to the greatest possible extent as the discomforts so greatly preclude one from enjoying the scenery – as it happened, there was not much in this line to enjoy till we reached the Kohallah Bungalow at 4.30 too worn out to have any thought above a cup of tea!

Punkahs were ordered and there we spent a hot night – the valley is so shut in, not a breath of air seems to stir there. The river still went rushing by and that alone seemed to be a thing alive, the steamy stillness being very oppressive.

Next morning we were ready and started at 6.30 for our 12 mile march to Dulai.

Immediately below the bungalow at Kohallah the river is spanned by a fine suspension bridge which joins British and Kashmir territory. Having paid our toll we crossed the Rubicon and felt we were really in the Happy Valley for the road follows the course of the river the whole way after this and the windings and deviations of the river made charming views at every turn round the face of the hill.

The river flows at the foot of hills which rise steeply from each side of it, towering high up to the skies on both sides yet covered with lovely green jungle, low, but varied.

The road is sometimes high above the river and you can look down and see two or three of its windings gleaming through the overhanging foliage, its rocky bed making the water foam and splash in quite an angry hill-torrent manner. We crossed numbers of small bridges thrown across ravines which are quite dry but so steep and rocky they must make lovely waterfall effects in the months of May and June when the snow of the surrounding hilltops is melting: there was no glimpse of snow to be had anywhere on this march. The road was good and fairly level, with rises and falls which were appreciable, such a contrast to the really trying march down to Kohallah the previous day.

We had some little excitement passing droves of bullocks – laden – which have the most wonderful faculty for taking a zig-zag course, no two following each other straight: we afterwards met droves of donkeys which were much easier to pass they kept so close together on the same side of the road. Camels again are our dread as they are worse than bullocks as they have a way of standing craning their necks about and one has to be on the alert to dive under their heads and trot past at the right moment. A steam roller too, took off our attention from the never-tiring scenery around.

At 10 a.m. we came in sight of a sweet little gabled bungalow, quite a little gem in the way of Bungalows, it was built in such a pretty shape, irregular, with a porch running out here and there with gabled roof and lattice work in portions of the verandah nicely painted, the verandah being ceiled with varnished, diagonally placed planks of wood.

The internal arrangements were on quite an elaborate scale, with English carpeting, colour washed walls with wooden wainscoting, varnished wooden shelves and mantelpiece with over-mantel of the same. The chairs and tables being so clean and fresh, the beds too looked quite inviting having a clean piece of canvas cloth stretched securely instead of the usual suspicious looking rewar – the dressing room was quite in keeping – in fact the little house, instead of being an object for the eye to avoid as a blot on the fair landscape is quite in keeping, being so picturesque itself.

The scenery seems to have inspired the builders and road makers as even the milestones are artistic; we left our solid English blocks of milestones on the other side and began numbering the miles afresh from 1 – the figure being placed on the topmost block of five blocks of stone with square corners set at angles to each other, graduated in size but as the uppermost block is only fixed by mortar it is apt to get dislodged and being the only serviceable part of the erection it would seem to have been wiser to have been less artistic, which strikes one forcibly when one comes to being the way worn traveller counting the weary miles, sitting in a rattling tonga, hot and flushed, covered with dust and growing gradually deaf with repeated calls of the tonga horn, necessary in the twistings and roundings of the tortuous stream, till they well nigh wish the Jhelum had run straight, they, being shut in all over by the hood have nothing to look at but the dusty roads <u>and</u> the milestones! We passed many tongas with occupants who exactly tallied with the above description, and we gloried in our freedom on horseback and more especially in going the opposite way to which they were. After spending the hottest part of the day at Dulai we started at 4.30 p.m. on our second afternoon march to Domel, 9 miles off – again I felt the disagreeableness of an *afternoon march. The valley widened during this march, the hills standing back after leaving a plateau at some 50 ft. above the river on which the country people had grown rice, evidently planted at different periods, as the effect of the ripening grain and the fresh green of the growing paddy was lovely in its variety giving such a bright touch to the sombre mountains in the evening light.*

The river widened here greatly, and its current seemed less swift. The road was fairly level but occasionally on the descent it was so steamy and hot we progressed but slowly our horses seeming to feel the heat. We walked two miles of the way which was a relief and reached Domel by dusk the daylight softening into moonlight till the whole place was bathed in the sweet cool light.

The Bungalow itself is a second Dulai on a larger scale – extremely comfortable – but the view here is quite the most charming we have had. There is a tiny, artistic little Pier run out from the bungalow into the River from the end of which one gets a lovely view of the meeting of the waters of the Kissengunga with the Jhelum, they both have swift currents and the effect of their meeting is joyous, such a gushing and tumbling and roaring in it making such beautiful white spray and then dashing on together with reunited force round the bend of the hill and yet not mingling, each river trying to hold its own as one can see in the different colouring, the one murky brown, the other blueish green, each having a race for life, but the stronger conquers and the little brown hill torrent succumbs and is absorbed and is lost in the flood of the other – and the grand old hills rise silent and strong and calm above all this swirling and noise looking more solemn in the moonlight which intensifies their great height and yet touches with such a pure silver, the rushing water giving the feeling that the light and joy of our Heavenly Father's love runs continuously through the graver moments of life and even through its deep shadows: reluctant as we were we had to leave the impressive scene and turn our thoughts to creature comforts – order punkah coolies and barricade ourselves against the intrusive pie-dogs which even in this sweet spot haunt the traveller with such perseverance.

A hot wakeful night resulted in a late start on the morning of the 17th. We passed through the little town in which the P.W.W. have placed their workshops, with hideous noisy engines sawing the beams and planks for the numerous bridges and for the protective palings of the road – the said palings by the way, being no protection or preventive to anything going over the edge, as they are put up so high with the struts so far apart and, if anything, <u>below</u> the edge of the road – a horse could slip away underneath with the greatest of ease as of course the hillside slopes away from under the paling and generally at a steep decline. Seeing the engines made us glad we had arrived at night when all was quiet. There was a bridge across the Jhelum here but we had not to cross again having to keep to our left bank of the river, but all the same they exacted a toll for simply passing the entrance to the bridge! The ways and means a native will descend to make money! tho' a Rajah. This march from Domel to Ghari was even more beautiful than the previous day, each turn of the road giving a fresh view of the river narrowing into more of a gorge and then widening out again with the hills standing back with gaps in the continuous range, showing glimpses of range upon range, some topped with a fringe of pine trees and others only clothed in grass with the red and purple soil showing through. The morning being cloudy and cool helped us to enjoy our ride, and the road allowing of a canter brought us to our destination earlier than usual.

The little bungalow lies on the road side immediately above the river and is still in the same style as the last two. The feature of the place I thought was the very curious and purely native rope bridge across the river, which was quite 50 ft. wide here and with a particularly swift current, and yet the natives walk over and cross each other in the middle of this very insecure looking tightrope. The bridge is composed of three ropes – two slung from two upright posts on a level with each other and stretched across to two other uprights on the opposite bank – the third rope is slung from a bar across the posts so as to drop in the middle of the other two ropes but about 5 ft. lower. On this single rope they place their feet, holding on to the upper two for support, the three ropes being kept somewhat in their relative positions to each other by V shaped sticks placed a few feet apart from each other. The nimble way in which the people go over, some carrying children, makes one giddy to watch. Miss Jacob went over it on the previous occasion when she passed Ghari, accomplishing the journey across without turning giddy, she took off her shoes and her guide told her to keep looking up – but even then the rushing torrent under this very transparent bridge would have been enough for most girls to have shrunk from and turned back, but she was plucky enough to go through with it – which meant coming _back_ too!

We could not post letters here tho' we wrote them, there was *certainly a State Post Office but hardly to be trusted, though you are expected to pay double postage on such letter for the privilege of entrusting your correspondence to a postmaster who has to be told by you in which direction your letters have to go – towards India or further into Kashmir! So the risk we considered too great for our valuable epistles and discarded the idea of using the State.*

It was much cooler here, tho' we still required punkahs – the night was fairly pleasant – this little bungalow seems much appreciated as it was quite full on the night we spent in it.

The next march of 10 miles was along a fairly level road. We left Ghari in excellent time, too punctually for our servants, whom we foolishly left behind and of course they followed at their leisure thus preventing us having a canter on the road, that happened on that day to be particularly suitable for fast going – but the feeling of annoyance could not well linger as the majesty of the grand old mountains seem to shame away our petty feelings making one feel how very small and puny man really is, and more so when giving way to human passion in any form. If only the feeling of elevation would stay! If one could only grasp and hold the influence that these mighty hills produce, it makes one think that perhaps the daily life lived so much on a level would be higher and better for the influence – but after all it is not outward things that ought to influence our higher nature or our strivings after a higher life. If they were all we trusted, how soon we should find we are building on sand.

The end of the 10 miles brought us to a wooden trestle bridge, somewhat picturesque which would have looked better if the wide rocky bed of its ravine had been full of water. As it was, there was a tiny streamlet meandering between the rocks, finding its way slowly to the river.

After crossing the bridge we looked down on the Bungalow of Hutian. What a cruel contrast to the previous three bungalows. Hitherto the travelling in Kashmir had been perfect fairyland, and here was a bungalow to which distance lent <u>no</u> enchantment! However, we turned off the road, dismounted, and began to walk down a zig-zag of a mountain torrent which, I was informed was the <u>old road</u> to Baramullah! Whereupon I blessed the fate that brought us to Kashmir in the days of the <u>new</u> road! We entered the verandah, which was just high enough to respect Miss Jacob's topi, and on looking round it appeared as if we had come to the back of the bungalow as there was a row of <u>batten</u> doors – but the resident Khansamah rushed forward and busily opened a door and ushered us into a barnlike place, the roof very little higher than the verandah. It was in such an uncertain condition, as if hesitating whether to yield to the force of gravitation or still to resist, and someone in sympathy with its efforts to resist, had placed an iron rail across but it still looked alarmingly unsafe. The walls were irregularly plastered and whitewashed and this was what we had been let down to with a run! However, when our servants arrived and we got out our different odds and ends the depressing effect wore off and we had a fairly cool day, lovely moonlight night – after which we left poor ugly old Hutian without a regret and started on our eleven mile march to Chakoti. This march contained the first element of danger we had experienced so far. The road ran along high up on the hillside with the river rushing and gurgling with a suppressed *roar at the foot of the valley where our hill dropped down to the waters' edge as steeply as it well could. The river here had narrowed considerably and had more of the mountain torrent about it, and we noticed that along this steep and really dangerous portion of the road the builders had, in sheer perverseness, used paling most extensively instead of the substantial parapet wall, which in most places gives at least a feeling of moral security. We passed a lovely little gushing waterfall with two falls. The little bridge across had to be placed so close to the fall that they had thought it necessary to erect a hoarding of planks, we concluded, for the purpose of preventing horses being startled by the rush of water, and yet on the other side where there was a sheer drop they had placed a rustic but very insecure paling of uncut logs of slender trees. Miss Jacob's horse refused it at first but when persuaded edged away from the hoarding too close to the paling for comfort. However, we reached our destination safely to find a bungalow, an improvement on Hutian tho' in the same style – this time it is <u>above</u> the road which in itself was an advantage. The view was very lovely there, being a plateau at the foot of the hill between us and the drop to the river, covered with the varied shades of green paddy. We are out of reach of the sounds of the grand old River, which has been in our ears every night since our joining it – but we still have the sound of running water, as there is a tiny streamlet trickling past our doors, clear as crystal and deliciously cool.*

We walked up a portion of the old road in the evening and tried to imagine what it would mean marching over the stony narrow pathway, and came to the conclusion, tho' it might give a more wild romantic air to the expedition, yet we would rather forego that and use the good broad new road. We gathered and pressed some beautiful specimens of very large leaved maiden hair ferns and leaves. The night passed in the Chikoti bungalow was pleasantly cool tho' storm clouds were hanging about but not heavy enough to obscure the lovely full moon, but rather to enhance the beauty of it.

We were ready in the morning of the 19th, Saturday, to start as usual at 6.30 but a heavy shower of rain came on and delayed us. When it stopped we began our march by walking about a mile, trying to save our horses if possible as their backs had got rubbed somewhat on the previous day – tho' not seriously.

I think I find each day's march more beautiful than the last – certainly this morning's was perfect in its impressive grandeur. The mountains closed in upon the River, hemming it in to a narrow gorge above which they towered in noble rocks steep, and resounding to the roar of the angry river dashing and foaming and struggling, racing to be free of the restraining rocks. The road ran high above the water which in some places was nothing but writhing foam, and in other places a clear sea green, the hills rising straight and high and the road turning round innumerable curves of the ravines up which one gets such lovely peeps of dark green depths. At the back of which again rise numbers of other hill tops, range after range, each seeming higher than the others, some bare of trees only clothed with a soft covering of grass while others are masses of deep foliage with sturdy pines standing erect on the highest peaks, pointing upward to the wonderful blue of the sky. And thus we came up this gorge-like portion of the Happy Valley having ample time to drink in all the beauty we passed through as we had to walk our horses the whole of the 14 miles – at the end of which we reached Uri where we intend spending our Sunday.

Our Sunday was a beautifully cloudy and cool day which was fortunate for our horses, as there were no stables here and no shade worth speaking of so they were saved the fierce sun, which is still exceedingly hot and our day passed pleasingly in reading and some writing. In the evening we took a stroll down a rocky little path into a ravine which was very beautiful. There was a rustic little bridge, rickety to an extreme, over a dear little clear babbling stream wandering among boulders and round two huge rocks, making such a sweet picture with the huge mountains towering above: the golden light the hills caught was so lovely, the sun setting somewhere out of sight, but the golden glow touching the hills. It was all very peaceful, the mountains looking so strong and steadfast.

Half past six on Monday morning saw us on horseback. The first 2½ miles took us into a deep ravine, each so far up it before it was narrow enough to be spanned by a bridge. By the time we had got back along the other side of the ravine and opposite the bungalow once more we found an hour had flown and as we thought we had 14 miles to do, we kept our horses at a steady walk of 4 miles an hour. For some miles we could do nothing but walk as the road had sharp and frequent curves and more on the decline than anything. We looked across the river at one time on to a small plateau where there were the ruins of a fine fort – the gateway still having portions entire tho' the whole was grass grown and looked as if it had seen much in life before dropping into its present decay. The road got steeper and we soon found ourselves quite close to the water's edge, the hills having receded and the road running along on a flat portion winding in and out of trees. On our right being masses of jungle with creepers and on our left the trees grew down to the water's edge, overhanging the water and fringing the bank. The River was much wider here, and being so open we could see some distance up it, the current was very swift and it still went rushing along with so much noise we could with difficulty hear each other speak.

We had a lovely view, especially at one part, where the river came round a curve into the open with a background of a towering rock whose shape and surface was all lost in a haze of deepest ultramarine blue. Some portions have deeper more mysterious shadows, especially low down near the river which looked so cool and white glancing round this curve with its spray and foam and in the foreground the bright greens and yellows of the woods with an occasional sombre fir or a tall spire of a pine tree varying it. The whole was beautiful and when we reached Rampur we quite thought it was the loveliest march we had had.

The Bungalow is situated on the roadside a little way off from the river but opposite a magnificent high rock face and promontories covered with fir trees, making a grand view. The Bungalow is at present under repairs but there are two suites of rooms available. It looks as if we should be the only occupants tonight, tho' we have not been alone at any of the bungalows yet. I mean without other Europeans. We gathered some brilliant red autumnal vine leaves this morning. The vines seemed to be over everything, especially over the pines, whose stiffness was much softened by the waving tendrils and shaped leaves all over them.

The horses were quite fresh after their Sunday's rest and went willingly and well – their backs are quite well again and they, with us, enjoyed the keen freshness there was in the morning air. During the day the bungalow filled up – with people returning from Kashmir.

Our days slip by very fast with writing, working and reading. The evenings we generally fill up with a stroll when we specially look out for pretty leaves or ferns which we press – not very successfully, as we have no box with us, so place the leaves in between newspapers and magazines and lay them under our <u>mattresses</u>! In the morning they are sufficiently pressed for us to lay in the portmanteau and next day repeat the process. The day spent in Rampur was beautifully cool and after a good night we rose at 5 a.m. starting at 6 on our 16 mile march. The poor horses are subjected to such erratic treatment, as the syces have no idea as to time in the night. I remember one night lying awake and looking out on the clear moonlight, I saw the syce get up, divide the morning grass and give it to the horses! I was surprised, so thought I better make sure of the time, and found it to be only ¼ to 2!

On the morning of Tuesday the 22nd we started on the final march of our ride. We had a glorious sunrise on the hill tops. At the back of us was an angry storm cloud but in front the sky was of the calmest most delicate tints imaginable, the softest pink on the tiny white clouds with a softening grey edge on palest blue melting into a green and lemon, and the rocks and hilltops all caught the rose tint until the colouring was sublime, till the storm clouds gained the ascendant and reflected an angry yellow gleam – then all died away and the morning turned grey, and after the first three miles (during which we had a canter) rain began to fall and continued steadily to the end of the remaining 13 miles. The scenery was still very beautiful tho' seen under the aspect of grey mist and clouds.

The river quite lost its nature of a mountain torrent here, changing into a wide open, calm, peacefully running river, still winding but not among the hills – they having receded, leaving the river wandering at will over a wide flat plain, forming little islands for itself with willows fringing them. The road ran all the way close to the river. We had many good level portions over which we cantered but the horses could not realize that their misery would be lessened and their comfort reached sooner the quicker they went. We at last reached Baramullah at a ¼ to 10 to find that the servants had been brisk and engaged two boats which Miss Jacob found to our surprise were the same that they had used when they came here last in May, so the men knew exactly how everything ought to be arranged, and we found the little living boat perfectly charming. It is so tiny and snug, with just enough room for the beds to stand beside each other with a tiny passage between, then a little table on one side at the foot of one bed and the space at the foot of the other bed was left for chairs and our bags. There is a little partitioned off dressing room and that is all our domain for the next 10 days.

The servants have a similar boat – our little dressing-room in their boat forming the kitchen.

The roof we were glad to find was strong and water proof, the walls being formed of grass chicks hanging all round, six to a side, hanging close together and able to be tied up at will – at night all

My great-grandfather Henry Bawn Addis - co-designer of the
Darjeeling Himalayan Railway. En route from Kashmir to Murree.

Vale of Kashmir.

Tibetan woman and child.

The Himalayas.

Vale of Kashmir.

The Jhelum river.

Murree.

Rope bridge.

being let down and another in the front by the prow, making everything most snug as we found when we moored the same night at a place called Sopor – a village of some size. The mosquitoes are something dreadful. They <u>swarm</u> but seem so drowsy they are easy to kill, but in doing so their number never seems to diminish.

The morning dawned cloudy and misty with a bit of a breeze, quite enough to prevent the boatmen venturing by the Wauler Lake route to Serinagur, so we started at 6 a.m. and soon found ourselves in an expanse of water reaching far on all sides of us but covered as far as you could see with green weeds. The Singara plant with its curious black, three horned nuts floating on the water. We passed through this broad expanse with a few hillocks rising out of it having a few fisherman's huts on them.

On stopping for breakfast (which was necessary as we had to get our food from the other boat) the boatmen all set to work picking Singara nuts to boil and eat. They picked huge basketsful for future consumption – we tasted some later on and at first taste pronounced them disgusting, but afterwards thought it a taste that would grow on one.

After this we were towed and poled into a channel which grew narrower and shallower till we thought we <u>must</u> stick fast, especially at the very sharp corners we had to turn, the men all towing along the bank where they sank knee deep in mud – black sticky mud. It was a long steady pull and it was a great relief when we got out once more into an open sheet of water and found ourselves in the beautiful clean calm River with mountains all round and a lovely calm sunshine over everything, and as it had remained cloudy all the day *we appreciated the sunlight.*

Three o'clock brought us just under a little hill which Miss Jacob recognised as being by the Lake Manisbal and at once asked the boatmen if we could not go and see the Lake – but they demurred saying this boat could not go as there was some wind and they were afraid – but a happy thought struck one of them and he suggested our going in a small boat from the Village to which idea we heartily agreed, and by 3.30 having partaken of afternoon tea we saw our tiny vessel ready for us. It is a canoe-shaped boat with room for four – a blanket was spread on the bottom of the boat which was flat, on which we took our seats facing each other, then the two boatmen sat at one end, each with a small paddle and off we went – first up a small ordinary Nullah with high mud banks for about ¼ of an hour then suddenly we turned into the Lake. There really is no describing its beauty. There ought to be a special vocabulary for Kashmir to help one to express the beauty one sees - all one's familiar words are so meagre and far behind what one feels.

This is a perfect little gem of a mountain lake, lying peacefully quite out of the highway. It is only about two miles long to 1 broad and has hills rising from it on all sides, its banks fringed with willows and water lilies, and here and there a tall poplar. On the right bank as you enter there is a tiny picturesque little village which exports lime from its hills; at the extreme end of the Lake there is a little grove of Chenaar trees and by its side an orchard and garden where dwells an old white-headed Fakir, looking so venerable with his long white beard, sitting close to the mouth of a cavern he has excavated for his burying, and where he sits and dispenses his favours to any visitors in the shape of a gift of the finest grapes and peaches one could see. These are specially noted even in this land of abundant fruit – he added rosy-cheeked apples and pears also to the gift and we came away feeling quite greedy over the fruit and yet it seemed such a shame to demolish the lovely luscious dainties. Once more we entered our little boat, where the water comes within two inches of the edge, and away we went again – this time round by the other side. And now I must remark upon the marvellous clearness of the water which was such a deep blue, in the depths of which we could see a perfect world of feathery green growth and long whip-like roots of the water lilies, and then again the reflection of the cloud flecked sky and the rocks down which a small waterfall was trickling, and above all the mighty silent watchers – the mountains.

As we returned on the other side of the Lake we passed what must have been a very large fort judging from the remains, which formed three long and broad terraces with bastions at the corners and only a small piece of the wall left. The abode of some old chieftain who could be very secure in this mountain retreat.

Our men paddled away in a brisk manner that brought us back to our boat by 6 p.m. under the light of a beautiful sunset. On one hand the hills black with the shadows of dense grey and black clouds with frayed edges looking so threatening – while on the other hand snow-capped pure mountains rising into a sky of the palest most delicate blue and on which soft tinted clouds rested lovingly, then above a deep blue sky with silver edges white fleecy clouds all about catching pink tints from the sun.

We moored that night above the bridge at Shuntal where we

passed numbers of gentlemen fishing from little boats. The little village looked very pretty with its wooden pile bridge at its entrance with some grand old Chenaar trees keeping guard over all. The Chenaar seems to be a tree peculiar to Kashmir. It is a tree that grows as large as an English oak with thick heavy foliage of most beautifully shaped leaves something like a plane tree; its shade is very deep and they grow in large groves and frequently singly on the river's banks.

Six a.m. on Thursday the 24th saw us on our final journey before reaching Serinagur – the fort of which came in sight at 9 o'clock after steady towing up the river. The boatmen's wives and children all helping in turn at the towing and poling – the women I have already seen certainly have beautifully refined clear-cut features with always a smile and pleasant look on them which lends them half their charm. They are short and of a sturdy make and dress picturesquely but <u>not</u> cleanly! Always wearing a small round turban-like cape over which they wear their chuddah – a long blouse-like gown completing their costume.

Three p.m. brought us to the entrance of the town of Serinagur which we did not get <u>through</u> till 6 p.m.! The town is built on both sides of the river, their communication being connected by seven wooden pile bridges which heighten the effect of the picturesque scene. The houses are built in all sizes and of irregular shapes, some with balconies over which vines have grown in the most delightful way.

The water is literally alive with boats going up and down, passing and re-passing, some bearing a human freight while others, laden with grass or melons or wood, keep up a perfect kaleidoscope effect.

At one time we could look both up and down the river for a good distance and at each end there was a background of hills some with stray patches of snow making a lovely picture, then a turn would bring Serinagur Fort into the background making quite another view in the shifting scene.

At last we got clear of the town by turning at right angles up a nullah and mooring on the banks of what is called the Chenaar Bagh – the Bagh being formed by groves of these beautiful trees with their enormous trunks standing up straight and tall with their lovely heavy foliage casting a deep shade on the glade of grass under them where numbers of tents of all sizes were pitched. A good number of boats were moored along here but we found a nice quiet and private place for ourselves – after which we went for a walk, first of course to the Post Office. Miss Jacob had seven letters and I? not one! We continued our walk into the Moonshi Bagh where the married quarters of the residents and others are situated. We had to walk across a good broad grassy plain where a game of polo was in progress, the square being lined by avenues of poplars looking very straight and stiff with their grey trunks and grey green leaves. Several Europeans were walking about quite in tourist fashion, some with simply sun topis yet others dressed in the height of fashion.

In the Moonshi Bagh are some little gems of houses all flowers and creepers with thatched roofs looking quite idyllic – their view being the lovely river upon which the reflection of the sunset caused a perfect golden glory as we passed, the sky later on turning into a huge volcano of lurid red in a wide gap between two heavy black clouds.

We found our horses had arrived safely after their march from

Baramullah, then wended our way home at dusk to our snug little boat – finding it even yet difficult to realize, having reached Serinagur and haunted with the disagreeable feeling of its not lasting long, that our homeward journey must begin in exactly a week's time and there is so much to do in this week!

We spent the next day, Friday, in shopping – starting after breakfast in a little boat with a mat top, rowed or rather paddled, by our boatman. It has no seats but we spread a rug on the flat bottom and took pillows which we placed against a board meant for a back and were paddled down to the city. We stepped out on to a set of steps leading to the water's edge and entered a narrow street on our way to the Bazaar.

We went first to a silver smiths who had a lovely collection of exquisite work. There were epergues, vases, teasets with trays, muffineers, brooches, bangles etc. etc. etc. in fact a most tantalizing display of pure white silver, lined with gilt. They had teasets made in the shape of the Kashmir firepots called Kaugris, and another shape for the same purpose called Kaugs, the latter is made in some metal for everyday use and the former in earthenware covered with basket work. The Kashmiris use them for warming themselves, filling them with lighted charcoal and then sitting down with them between their knees, their blankets all over them forming a tent. The silver smiths had also made brooches and charms in the shape of the Kashmiri grass shoe – it is a sort of sandal which the men use made of grass. All the wares were most tempting but oh! for the wherewithal to invest in some! We bravely turned our backs on them and once more stumbled down the dark, dirty, winding little staircase that had brought us up to such a surprising display of purity and light.

We set off next to the coppersmiths guided by our boatmen who made a way for us through the crowded bazaar, we got through quite comfortably without any inconvenience and were very much struck with the absence of offensive odours – another groping up some steep steps and we were led into a room full of carved copper – beautiful work and of a lovely burnished colour. They also had teasets, vases etc. but what I specially admired were the tables – octagon in shape, the legs and frame made of carved walnut wood and the top of a lovely copper tray – an exquisite ornamental tea-table.

Here we were more able to spend the contents of our limited purses, and left – proud possessors of Kashmir work.

Then we had the papier-mache work to look at and were introduced to a tiny room rich with exquisite work – tables – milking stools – brackets, letter cases, racks and paper knives being the direction in which they displayed this art. There were numbers of patterns in numerous shades and colours – the black and gold Chenaar leaf pattern more particularly taking my fancy.

Some artist (English) sojourning in Kashmir had drawn pictures of the heads of all kinds of Shikar to be found and given them to the papier mache man who reproduces them on tables and other things with exquisite care and good taste but of course it is not <u>*native*</u> *art, but would delight the heart of a sportsman.*

We then went to the little stalls in the bazaar square, and bought odds and ends in the way of beads and curious bangles and lastly invested in 2 lbs of the best grapes (after Manisbal) to be seen, both purple and white for 2 annas! and descending to our waiting boat *were paddled home again, lounging in most luxurious fashion on our pillows, regaling ourselves with grapes – oh! Kashmir life is the ideal life! when pure physical enjoyment is sufficient. Fancy being able to shop in a native bazaar firstly by <u>boat</u> with no jolting, dust or noise, simply gliding along with only the sound of the gentle lapping of the water, then being able to pass in and out of a thick crowd of natives without a push or roughness of any kind, and above all <u>no smells!</u> everyone being as polite as could be – this to two unmarried girls.*

Our early morning walk we had taken up the Takt-i-Suliman (Solomon's Throne) a steep hill rising from the river's brink on the summit of which is now built a Hindoo Temple and from which a perfect panoramic view of Serinagur City and of the Jhelum river can be had. We were fortunate in having a beautifully clear day and could see <u>seven</u> windings of the river which has wound itself through the country in bold sweeps – like a serpent gleaming through its wooded banks. On the flat plain and in the distance range upon range of strong hills backed again by high jagged peaks of the pure eternal snow – then on the other hand the City, stretching for miles along each bank of the river and on all sides of it – water, the Dhal Lake stretching, a beautiful expanse of blue water and the canals and nullahs all about. Surely a veritable Venice of the East.

On the banks of the river just below us were the European Quarters, the Residency standing in the centre of its large garden with its neat little Lodge and the gates, and then the large grassy plain divided into squares by the poplar avenues, in the shade of which the residents enjoy walks and drives and rides.

Saturday we spent on the Dhal Lake, which we went to in our

214

small boat again. The Lake is large, surrounded by mountains fringed with the grey green of willows and the deep massive green of fine Chenaars, with villages dotted about on its banks, and some pleasure gardens of the Rajahs at different points. One we visited – the Shalier Bagh – which is an extensive garden with a canal running up the middle, dry at the time we saw it, with terraces thrown across, of masonry on splendid black polished marble pillars, the roof which they upheld being painted and finished in thorough native style – the tawdry contrast being quite painful, the pillars looked so thoroughly good. In front of these terraces were places for fountains and ornamental water. We stayed here for our breakfast which we ate in true picnic style under a large mulberry tree.

On entering the Dhal we noticed a number of long poles standing straight up out of what appeared to us to be banks – and on asking what they were for, were informed that the earth and grass we saw were <u>floating</u> islands the earth being only about a foot deep and they were kept in place by the long poles in order to anchor them from floating across the channels. Grass grows on all sides to the height of about 8 ft. and boatloads of it were going out. They use it for all the chicks and roofs of the boats – in fact the Dhal seems to be most lucrative to the State as we were told that as much as a seer (2 lbs) and a half in <u>gold</u> is made every day from what passes through the Dhal Ka Dharwaza (Gate of the Dhal).

We spent two days in Serinagur and then started back again to Sopor to leave the boat there and go up to see Gulmerg – this time our return journey to Sopor was through the Wauler Lake, as the Channel up which we had come had dried up. This lake is the largest in India and is quite a small sea surrounded by mountains and a grand old snow-capped peak called 'Hermac' keeping guard over all in silent grandeur. Of course our boatman detailed, for our encouragement, all the most fearful storms and disasters that had occurred on this Lake as it is subject to sudden squalls – being more than 8 miles long makes it very dangerous – however, we got across in safety and in daylight.

On Tuesday morning we had some trouble in starting, getting coolies and our baggage tat started, the Chowkidar of the town being specially troublesome. Our horses were on the other side of the village and we had to walk through its winding little streets of wooden houses and crossing the river by a bridge under which we saw some gentlemen fishing. We reached our horses and started.

Our way at first lay through rice fields all fast ripening and often crossing little brooks and streams so beautifully clear with rustic little bridges over them.

We ascended gradually and came to grassy hillocks with wild pear-trees dotted about laden with wild pears, which we gathered as we rode under them. They had more of the flavour of an English pear but were also astringent tho' juicy. I could not manage to eat more than two or three. Then we came to a lovely jungle of bushes and rose-bushes with their rich scarlet hips in bunches over them, then the walnut trees were a sight for shade. They grew so wide spreading and with their wide leaves, it was lovely under them.

Having gone on so for about 12 miles we came upon the servants making breakfast ready in the shade of a perfect grove of walnut trees, with beautifully green grassy terraces under them.

Having finished breakfast and gathered some fresh walnuts we again started on our ride, the pathway ascending rapidly till we came to very steep places with loose stones scattered all over. The horses went up with a will and with frequent rests for breath or for drinks at the streams. When we reached a part that was only a gradual ascent up the hillside with nothing but pines and firs above and below us, and this continued till we reached Gulmerg. The pathway was only about 3 ft. wide and in some places made one feel a little queer as there were no railings, and the hill ran away in a sheer drop without a tree. The gaps in the trees gave us glorious views of the Plains below with its Wauler Lake and River backed by ranges of hills, and they again bounded by a lovely range of everlasting snow – one peak being specially high made us conclude it was Nunga Purbet (Naked Mountain) which is 27,000 feet high.

We had not seen this range of hills before as we were too near the foot of the near range when on the River, and were always somewhat disappointed at not seeing more snow – but we have since been well repaid for our waiting.

Our entrance into Gulmerg was a charming surprise. We came to a point where two spurs nearly met and passing through their gap came in sight of an undulating plain of lovely green grass about 2 miles in extent, with the hills rising on all sides of it with pines and firs forming a wide belt round, above which rose another range of hills with patches of snow in among the pines and on the tops of the little hillocks were the most charming of little huts, more like the pictures one sees of Swiss Chalets among pines than anything else I could think of. These little huts are built of logs with the bark left on in its original roughness and then planks here and there which formed a good contrast to the rough bark, the whole view forming as beautiful a picture as could well be imagined. Seeing the snow lying apparently low down in the ravines we were at once fired with the determination to reach it – and after finding an empty hut and establishing ourselves in it we went to sleep with orders having been given for a coolie and a cold breakfast to accompany us the following morning up to the snow.

Gulmerg is practically empty – there seems to be <u>one</u> hut occupied and the occupants are on the eve of leaving. There is no bazaar or Post Office so we are right away up in the clouds with nothing but dear old nature, whose company we thoroughly appreciate!

We discovered our hut had no window in the frames and the cold night wind aroused all our ingenuity and we managed with sundry shawls and towels, out of the limited number brought with us, to modify the keenness of the wind – then two out of the three doors in the room we occupied would not keep shut and finding it necessary to protect ourselves from the inroads of the inevitable pariah dog we placed our beds against them and then retired to rest with huge fire of cones and pine wood crackling merrily.

Next morning, Wednesday the 30th, saw us on the way up to the snow. After crossing the meadow to reach the opposite slope, we at once began climbing the steep hillside in the shade of the grand old firs which opened unexpectedly into another lovely little meadow or <u>merg</u> just like the one we had left below, with a clear streamlet running through it and pines and firs all round and this we found occurred repeatedly and is quite a characteristic of the Kashmir hills and it is in these meadows on the hilltops that grow all the lovely *flowers one hears of as growing in such quantities – balsams, gentians and anemones, and numbers of other wild flowers, growing in such profusion as to form a perfect carpet of colour. Of course the season is passed for these and now they are these grass meadows where people graze their cattle in droves.*

We found, after two hours of steady climbing, that we had reached the upper edge of the belt of fir forest and above us rose a grassy mountain where lay the goal of our ambition – the <u>snow</u>!!

Choosing a shady knoll we left our coolie with the basket and continued our walk which was more of a scramble over boulders through a short thick little jungle and finding it grow steeper and steeper each step becoming more of an effort till <u>three quarters</u> of an hour later brought us to the bed of frozen <u>snow</u>! We scraped and ate it to our heart's content, glad of the drink of the refreshingly cool water of the stream which issued so pure and clear from under the snow. The view we had was glorious and with regret we turned back, feeling more than ever the greatness of our God 'For that Thy word is near thy wondrous works declare'. Truly a place where 'every prospect pleases and only man is vile' – one's own <u>littleness</u> and impurity of sinfulness always comes over one with such force when the grandeur of such a scene speaks so plainly of the Infinite Power and Wisdom of our Holy and yet <u>Loving</u> God. I think it certainly gives one a lift up as the sense of <u>adoration</u> is so strong.

Well, we turned and reached our breakfast taking nearly as long coming down as going up, the hillside was so rough, each step needed care – but we had really reached the line of perpetual snow.

We enjoyed our breakfast of duck and scones – cake and grapes! Ducks are absurdly cheap, this one being one of <u>four</u> I had bought *for 14 annas! ready for table. We came down again and reached our hut at 3 o'clock, having been on our feet since 9 o'clock, both climbing and descending with half an hour's rest for breakfast.*

After a rest and tea we went out for a stroll in the evening. I, quite coming to the conclusion there must be something revivifying in the air for us not to be too tired.

It was dusk before we returned and then we found we had lost our way! Finding ourselves at the Bazaar again after thinking we were on the point of turning into our own hut. We wandered about and fortunately came across a familiar landmark and then our syces' fire guided us to our temporary home.

Next morning we went for a good gallop round the race course, which the horses enjoyed as much as we. The weather is cloudless and mild and we think one could hardly conceive of a more beautiful place than this. It is nice too that it is new to Miss Jacob as well, for she did not come <u>here</u> on her previous visit with her parents.

After breakfast we were out again to 'explore', bringing our writing, and this thick production is the result of having to put up with a quill pen to write with when sitting in the shade of a mighty pine, with the wind soughing gently through its branches and an important woodpecker keeping up a busy tick-tack on the bark.

On our return to the hut after the above, we had tea and a rest, and then started again for a walk in another direction, coming back at nightfall quite satisfied with our two days' stay in Gulmerg.

The Kashmiris about are very simple and nice. We passed some making butter at the foot of a pine. They live out in the woods in little huts made of nothing better than <u>bark</u> cut off the enormous trunks of the firs in great plates and simply laid against each other *with fir branches across the top. A most frail looking habitation but easily removed to where their cattle need to graze. During the night of Thursday 1st October it began to rain and a regular wind and thunder storm set in – but it cleared by the time we had to start in the morning, on foot, with our coolies and horses following, by a different road from the one by which we had gone up to Gulmerg. This one was to bring us straight to Rampur, thereby saving a march to Baramullah and from that place to Rampur.*

We found the road very hard work. It was nothing but steep ascents and descents which grew more and more slippery as the rain began to fall and continued without cessation the whole day. After hours of slipping and scrambling we reached a cowherd's hut where our servant had managed a hot breakfast for us. Up to this we were unable to mount our horses, the road being quite unfit. We were soaked <u>through</u> and were right glad of the shelter, the good fire <u>with</u> its smoke and the floor covered with fir branches.

There was a log in it on which we sat and I, having divested myself of my boots and stockings, wrung the latter out and hung them to dry, then ate our breakfast feeling very grateful to our man for having made the effort of getting us a hot meal and good tea.

After spending half an hour here and being refreshed – the servants and coolies with their food and a smoke, and the horses with their grass – we all started again quite hopefully, thinking that the worst was over and that a descent of about 2 hours would bring us to Rampur, but alas! we were sadly mistaken, and found ourselves going up and down in the old way, but this time on grassland out of the forest. After an hour of this with clouds and mist and rain shutting us in closely, we came to a sudden descent – the pathway narrowing and going sheer down the hillside, in fact only a coolie track. It looked impossible for the horses and they, poor creatures, trembled from head to foot with fear as they were urged down over roots and trunks of fallen trees. Sometimes standing above a 4ft drop with nothing to land on but boulders or logs of fallen trees. No wonder they shrank from it poor things, urged over steep ground slippery with black mud or yellow clay – all four legs slipping from them at every step, the syces holding on bravely and encouraging the poor things. We hardly dared look back at them, dreading either of the horses going over the edge and carrying the syce with him down the awful slope – and thus we went on for hours slipping, stumbling, climbing and wading through mountain streams – with pelting rain, vivid lightning and crackling thunder till 5.30 p.m. when we reached the high road all safe without any accident to the men or horses, coolies or ourselves, and a great feeling of thankfulness to our Heavenly Father for His protecting care.

We found we had got <u>another</u> 5 miles to go before reaching the Bungalow so trudged on, soaked to the skin but keeping up a good pace tho the road was in some places over our ankles in water.

Darkness came on and still we persevered, seeing our way by flashes of lightning till an hour and a quarter brought us to the Bungalow, to find it full! But we had fallen into the hands of good Samaritans. General de Bourbol and a young officer occupying one room came out and invited us to their fire – then they disappeared and on appearing again brought with them a Dr. Dean who took us to his room and fire, wrapped us in blankets and sat us down to the dinner that was ready apparently for the three to dine together. He gave us scalding tea to drink and hurried the food into us and did everything he could to refresh us. By the time we were finished we found the other two gentlemen had vacated their room for us and we quickly availed ourselves of their kindness, and hastened to get off our dripping garments – dry the least wet things of our bedding and get to bed, thankful for the many mercies we had been the recipients of that day.

The servants and horses got shelter in a cowshed, the Bungalow stables being full.

Next morning, Friday, found us stiff after our 24 mile walk, but nothing worse for our wetting and fatigue. We dried as many things as possible in the fresh breeze that had sprung up; the rain having stopped we had our breakfast, then thought the best thing to do was to push on while it was fine. Laddie, our black horse Miss Jacob is riding, had got a swelling at the girth but that was all. It was wonderful that they were neither of them lame or strained in any way. Miss Jacob walked the whole of the 13 miles of that march to Uri, the last four miles in pouring rain – the road being very heavy in places from the landslips from the hill above.

I walked four miles of the march as the stiffness was bad after the previous day's walk and then rode, Miss Jacob quite refusing to ride and go shares in the one horse. It has rained steadily all last night and today Sunday the 4th October, we fortunately intended remaining here for today but hope it will clear for our journey tomorrow.

We are in a room without a fireplace which makes it rather comfortless as so many of our things are still wet, but we are glad to have got a room at all – as the rest of the Bungalow is quite full. The hills round about have a sprinkling of snow upon them but very light. There is not much to be seen of the hills at all as the clouds are very low. The servants are quite well which is a comfort. They have none of them complained of fever or anything; perhaps it is because we have been through exactly the same predicament as they – without house room or fire. My spaniel Skipper, who has gone bravely through the country with us, has gone stiff in two legs with all the cold and damp poor fellow.

We had to make room for two lady travellers who arrived during Sunday and it turned out that they were acquaintances. We all started again on Monday, the weather having cleared and our homeward journey was accomplished without any more rain and without anything untoward happening.

We reached Murree on Saturday the 10th doing the last 12 miles in a dandy (which is a sort of chair slung on poles carried by 4 men) having settled up all accounts satisfactorily – Miss Jacob and I exactly taking half share in all expenses, each share coming to 138 rupees only, after paying four servants, 2 ekkahs, Boats, Living, horses and an excursion to Gulmerg with stores – so thought that our month's little tour on horseback had been a thorough success and ending satisfactorily in every way.

We have been highly amused at the many exclamations we have been met with at our fathers having allowed us to go on such a wild trek all by ourselves!

Emma Helen Leslie

NOTE: Some words in the diary have had to be omitted because they were illegible; there are also some words or phrases whose meaning is now unclear. These have been reproduced without comment.